MW00813950

Identity Designed
The Definitive Guide to Visual Branding

David Airey

ROCKPORT

Inspiring | Educating | Creating | Entertaining

Brimming with creative inspiration, how-to projects, and useful information to enrich your everyday life, Quarto Knows is a favorite destination for those pursuing their interests and passions. Visit our site and dig deeper with our books into your area of interest: Quarto Creates, Quarto Cooks, Quarto Homes, Quarto Lives, Quarto Drives, Quarto Explores, Quarto Gifts, or Quarto Kids.

© 2019 Quarto Publishing Group USA Inc.
Text © 2019 David Airey

First published in 2019 by Rockport Publishers,
an imprint of The Quarto Group,
100 Cummings Center, Suite 265-D, Beverly, MA 01915, USA.
T (978) 282-9590 F (978) 283-2742 QuartoKnows.com

Rockport Publishers titles are also available at discount for retail, wholesale, promotional, and bulk purchase. For details, contact the Special Sales Manager by email at specialsales@quarto.com or by mail at The Quarto Group, Attn: Special Sales Manager, 100 Cummings Center, Suite 265-D, Beverly, MA 01915, USA.

10 9 8 7 6 5 4 3 2

ISBN: 978-1-63159-594-3

Digital edition published in 2019
eISBN: 978-1-63159-595-0

Library of Congress Cataloging-in-Publication Data is available

Design and Page Layout: David Airey
Cover Typeface: Avenir Next
Interior Typefaces: New Hero, New Rubrik Edge, and Alegreya
Photography courtesy of each design studio, or as indicated.

Printed in China

Contents

Introduction

"As a rule, the experienced designer does not begin with some preconceived idea. Rather, the idea is [or should be] the result of careful observation, and the design a product of that idea."

— Paul Rand

Photos from Unsplash (clockwise from top left) by Samuel Zeller,
Mark Kucharski, and Quino Al. Previous page by Joao Tzanno.

The origins of identity design began in the times of the earliest human tribes. Consider how members of a tribe would distinguish themselves from other tribes by markings, dances, language, and other visual and verbal signs. Knights and nobility, villages, cities, and countries—they, too, were all given a form of differentiating visual mark.

What began as a manifestation of the human condition evolved into something else in the realm of commerce—ancient Egyptians branded their cattle with hot irons to signify ownership, and potters engraved their makers' marks on bowls and plates as a guarantee of quality.

When the difference between two functionally similar products is minimal, there's a need to create an emotional differentiation, wherein lies the roots of identity design in relation to consumer products and services. In 1876, the Trade Mark Registration Act was passed in the United Kingdom, and Bass Ale was the first trademarked brand in the world. This act gave businesses the ability to protect their identifying marks from use by competing companies and, coupled with the growth in commerce after the Industrial Revolution, opened the door to the spreading of brands across the globe. The oldest U.S. trademark still in use is that of Samson slaying a lion, issued to the Samson rope company in 1884.

A visual identity is to business what faces are to people, and although it was once relatively simple to create different marks for competing businesses, the advance of capitalism has challenged designers to craft distinction in highly saturated worldwide markets. It's a challenge that brings opportunity and responsibility. Good businesspeople know the value that design can have on their brands, and whereas it was previously more common for designers to find themselves in meetings with middle managers, they're now often an integral part of the boardroom, advising owners and CEOs on how to succeed.

Symbolism is generally the first thing that comes to mind when people think about a brand's visual identity—e.g., the swoosh, red cross, golden arches, and bitten apple. It's also just one small piece of the picture. In the words of Brian Collins, "Brands exist in the minds of people who interact with them," and while memories of a brand are driven by the quality of a product or service, the quality is increasingly being backed up by a range of designed elements that are appropriate to what's on offer. A brand's identity can include a logo, website, vehicle graphics, business cards, staff uniforms, sound branding, tone of voice, packaging, art direction, mannerisms, and a lot more.

Consider what a potential customer might see, or hear, or even smell, or feel, when lifting a product off a shelf, using a digital service, or climbing up the steps onto a plane. Signage, reception desks, carrier bags, invoices, receipts, social media profiles, language, photography, typefaces in marketing literature—these are all parts of the broader identity. Although some companies have an enormous number of items that can be branded, good design doesn't need to be complicated. Rather, the strongest design includes only as much as what's necessary.

Not every customer is a designer, but we're all surrounded by design, and whether or not we're aware of it, the ways in which a brand is packaged offer clues to its quality. How a product or service looks must reflect the quality of what's on sale. When it doesn't, there's a disconnect between what a buyer sees and the impression the seller wants to give. Equally, people are smarter than to keep buying something that sets expectations higher than what's

Photos from Unsplash (clockwise from top left)
by Leio McLaren, Yoann Siloine, Hello I'm Nik,
Antonio Molinari, and Luis Cortes Martinez.

delivered. The creation of a fitting brand identity is an investment that can pay off year after year, with a continual increase in value because the more people see a design, the faster they remember it the next time they need the associated product or service.

Consistency is often wrongly associated with sameness, but it can mean consistently distinctive and vibrant.

Great brands are consistent. The same is true of their identities. Consistency is often wrongly associated with sameness, but it can mean consistently distinctive and vibrant. That can be achieved simply by using a single typeface in a variety of ways, combining a distinctive palette with compelling copy, crafting a more extensive unit of complementary elements, and myriad other ways that help to visually ingrain a brand experience to memory.

When used correctly, design helps to turn potential buyers into loyal customers and advocates,

and this book has been written to document what's involved in the creation of strong, emotive, and enduring identities. After reading, you'll be able to apply the same principles and techniques to your own projects or business ventures.

I'm David Airey, and since starting my independent design studio in 2005, I've specialized in designing identities for companies of all sizes around the world. Despite my years of experience focusing on the topic of this book, the majority of my time in the profession has seen me work independently rather than as part of a larger firm. Although that's helped me to learn about the business of design much quicker than I otherwise would have, it's also meant that I've been less likely to change my ways—to fix what isn't broken, at least from my perspective.

From talking to the hundreds of designers I've made friends with over the years, it's clear that there's no single set of rules that eclipses all others when crafting the right brand identity. So instead of writing about how I conduct business, I spent months interviewing a variety of the world's most talented designers and studios about the processes they follow when helping their clients to achieve their goals. The result is an intriguing insight into how visual identity work is carried out by design firms in the United States, Canada, England, Scotland, Sweden, Belgium, Ukraine, Vietnam, Singapore, and Brazil. The contributing studios reveal their design process from start to finish, sharing a detailed overview of how they work with clients, as well as walking you through one of their most compelling projects. At the end of each feature, I've added a brief recap to highlight important points.

Thank you for joining us.

"Design has to work.
Art does not."

Donald Judd

Case studies

SWEAT
IT OUT

Lantern

London
www.lanternlondon.com

Project: Primal Roots

Primal Roots is a woodland-based fitness and well-being boot camp rooted in the pursuit of both external and internal strength, endurance, and natural movement. Working closely with homeless charities and local authorities, it offers fitness training to help the recovery of those who would otherwise not have access to such services.

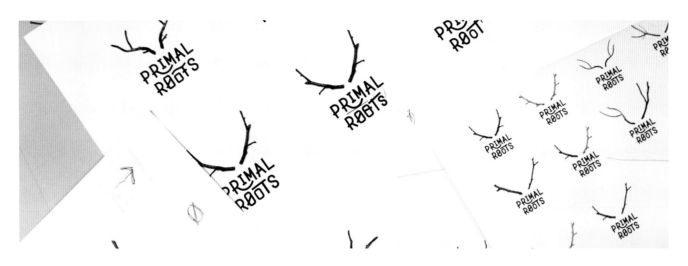

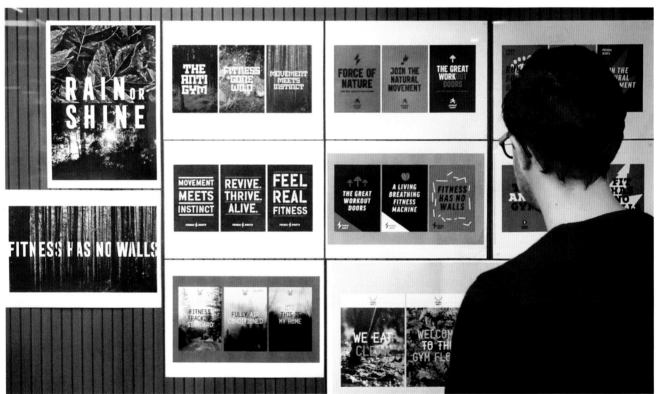

A lot of what we do is based upon the messaging and
the attitude, character, and personality of the brand.

When we're approached by clients, we always start with a quick call or face-to-face meeting to get a sense of why they do what they do, who their audience is, and what they're trying to achieve. We need to have that conversation, regardless of whether we go on to collaborate. Depending on the quality of the inquiry and the amount of information we're given, we can get a sense of whether they'll fit with what we generally charge for the work. We could waste a lot of each other's time if we go through the proposal stage and they've only got £100 ($130) to spend on a logo.

Rather than asking a specific set of questions, we try to get an understanding of the business, the ambitions for the project, and the key deliverables. We normally discuss the process of one of our previous projects—the brief, the creative routes we presented, the route the client chose, and the guidelines we developed. Sometimes it's difficult for people to grasp the tangible items they'll get at the end, so rather than just show them five nicely Photoshopped projects, we make it about the process and how we get to the end point.

Early conversations with Primal Roots were more straightforward than normal because we'd already worked with them on another social enterprise called Growth Rings. So, they had an idea of how we work and what we tend to charge, but our proposal still went into detail on the cost breakdown, process, and deadlines to help convince everyone we were the right fit. We did our due diligence on the company, too, because we weren't familiar with everyone involved.

Project deliverables
We were hired for the naming, branding, and positioning, and for providing strategic insight to help promote their holistic approach to everyone from local authorities and healthcare commissioners to the general public. We position ourselves as the brand attitude agency, and our selling point is that we focus a huge amount of the process on tone of voice and creative messaging so our clients come away with a suite of ten to fifteen powerful phrases that speak to their audiences in the most appropriate way. The verbal side of a brand is as much a part of things as the visual, so one of the key deliverables was that library of creative messages.

The verbal side of a brand is as much a part of things as the visual.

The brand development included two different design routes from which the client could choose, and we delivered logo artwork, guidelines, and sample applications, such as what an ad or brochure cover would look like. Although the client might not necessarily run a traditional ad, our sample applications can still be used, for example, in the form of a post on social media, where an image of a billboard or a brochure cover is uploaded.

The company came to us known as Nature's Gym. We renamed the brand as Primal Roots to give it a bit more attitude. Nature's Gym was very functional, and although it positioned what the brand is about,

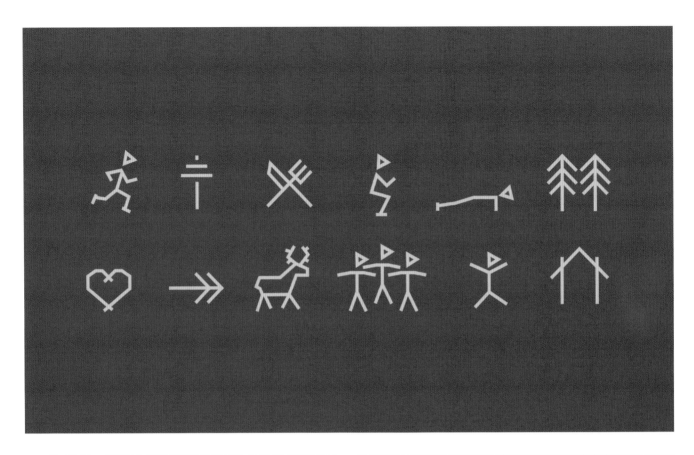

Relevant iconography helps to create a more cohesive identity even in the smallest of applications.

Primal Roots is much more about the emotional side. There was also the challenge around using the word "gym" because some of the audiences don't like them.

We launched their Squarespace website, and set up their Twitter and Instagram profiles with header images and avatars, before preparing social media posts to kick things off.

Design pricing

We charged £10,000 ($13,000) for the Primal Roots work. That's significantly less than we normally price those deliverables, but we tend to reduce our rate for one or two special interest projects each year, such as charities or social enterprises. We try to work with people who we know are prepared to take their brand in a brave direction, or where we think there's a real value in the business itself. It depends on an individual basis who we work with at that price, otherwise we'd not make any money.

We set our prices based on the time it will take to create the deliverables. Timing is often driven by a deadline, such as when a client might have an event to prepare for or launch a website by. One of the challenges with being a designer is that if you're particularly passionate about a project, and if there's a specific execution you really want to do that might take twice as long, you embrace that as part of the process.

For some projects we might suggest an illustrative route that needs to be done externally, which can affect the timing. Obviously, there's an additional cost for the client, too. We caveat that in our terms—illustration, photography, and so on will be extras if required.

For a typical identity project, we estimate it takes about ten to twelve weeks to deliver brand guidelines. The amount of time can vary greatly depending on how many stakeholder reviews need to happen. We've had projects that lasted eighteen months due to the number of people involved in the project reviews. So, we give our initial estimate, but we also mention factors that might affect the duration—e.g., a decision maker being unavailable for a week or two.

As a design firm, be mindful of the value you offer as you grow in credibility and awareness. With a back catalogue of great references, we've increased our rates year after year since opening our doors. It can be tricky if you've worked with a client in the past and they come back and want a similar job done, or they've recommended you to someone and told them how much they paid, but that's something you just have to deal with.

If a client ever wants the price reduced, we'll reduce what we deliver instead. Perhaps certain clients don't need as comprehensive a guidelines document, or they can get someone local to create their social media assets once we've developed the branding. Occasionally we might hear that the client wants to see one creative route instead of two. So we negotiate based on the deliverables. We won't arbitrarily say, "Okay, we'll do it for that price," because we'll get caught in a cycle and it'll happen on every project. There's a risk of existing clients recommending you to someone where the same thing happens.

Some studios charge based on value, but with the type of clients we work with that's quite a hard sell. It would be nice to be in a position to do that, but even then, to a certain extent the value you offer is based on the time you put into a project.

We won't begin the creative work until a down payment has been made. If we see benefit in the project, then when we put together a proposal, we

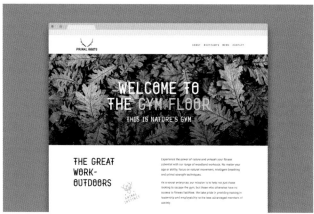

Our clients come away with a suite of ten to fifteen powerful messages that relate to their audiences in the most appropriate way.

might include a page or two about the brands we think are interesting to discuss in a workshop and what we can learn from them—but we never start creative development until payment is made.

Terms and conditions

Our draft terms came from an online template to help with the foundations. Once we built in specifics relevant to our own process and payment terms, we had the document checked by a legal professional who offered some suggestions.

We won't begin the creative work until a down payment has been made.

After any initial chat with a potential client, we'll prepare and email a proposal with the terms and conditions at the back. Our email will say something along the lines of, "If you'd like to progress with the project, we just need you to confirm in writing that you're happy with the proposal and the terms in the document." We accept their agreement via email and, at that point, we need the initial payment that's outlined in the proposal before we start work.

We accept payment through bank transfer. You can use PayPal and, in theory, take payment by card, but that doesn't sit well with us as a service-based business. You can devalue what you're doing that way. We always ask to be billed in pounds, regardless of where our clients are based, as it makes things easier for our accounts.

Perhaps once or twice a year, we encounter issues with clients either not paying, or paying late. It's never an issue of the work being disliked. It's usually the business struggling financially and they simply can't afford to pay.

We request 50 percent of our fee up front, with the remaining 50 percent due at the end. With larger projects, we tend to divide the second 50 percent into more than one payment, reducing the risk on that final installment. Anytime something has gone wrong, it's with the end payment. That's the harder one to chase.

We typically don't provide logo artwork until the final payment is made, but that doesn't mean that a client can't start producing collateral before we're fully paid. They have a guidelines document and, if they wanted, they could open the document in Illustrator and get around potential password locks. It's difficult to control. So our terms state that the copyright doesn't transfer to the client until final payment is made. If they start using what we've designed on their website or social media, for example, there's an additional right to chase them because they're identifying themselves with work they don't own. We stipulate an interest rate for late payment, which is the bank base rate plus 3 percent. That's pretty standard. With other design firms, that rate can typically range from 3 to 8 percent.

Although it's rare, we have had payments that were delayed by more than a year, resulting in the addition of our interest fee. In such a case, we would break down the cost and begin a six-month

We needed to speak to quite a range of people, and the task was
to understand what the "pain points" were for each group.

payment plan. There's only been one instance when that didn't work and we had to go in the direction of the small claims court to get what we were owed. It's easy to do online, but the client agreed to pay as soon as legal proceedings were put into motion, so thankfully it was settled before it got to that stage. Having our terms and conditions definitely helped in that scenario. Additionally, we had written confirmation that the client wanted to initiate the project and that they accepted they were late in paying, so there was a considerable amount of back-and-forth written communication.

The audit, workshop, and brief

After receiving a down payment, in a typical identity project, we audit the client's brand so we've got an in-depth understanding of what they're about, what their sector's about, who their competitors are, and how they're marketed. Once we're done with the audit, we'll hold a workshop, not only with the people involved in the business, but also with the beneficiaries. For Primal Roots that meant inviting homeless people to the workshop to talk about their experiences of the fitness boot camp. We did the boot camp sessions, too, to give a more complete understanding.

In the workshop, we'll discuss best-practice brands, either in the same or a similar sector. For Primal Roots, these brands included Nike and Fitness First—companies with strong positioning in terms of what they stand for. It's about getting the client excited about the future vision of their business. It also helps if we can just get the client to say, "Oh no, I don't like that brand," because it gives a clearer sense of what they want to achieve.

People generally don't mind going to the gym and exercising, but when it's outside and freezing cold or pouring with rain—as is sometimes the case with Primal Roots—that's another challenge. We discuss these "pain points" with the client, talking about how we can turn a potential negative into a positive that people will embrace. With outdoor exercise, you think that even though it's going to rain, it's going to be amazing because you're going to feel that sense of relief and escapism, benefits you won't ordinarily get in a gym.

Following our audits and workshops, we put together the creative brief that the client needs to agree upon. For Primal Roots, the brief included an introduction to the client business, the project objectives, the sector context, the health benefits, and that outdoor exercise is much more beneficial than exercising in a gym. Also included is the client vision and their different audiences—Primal Roots had to appeal to charities and healthcare commissioners, as well as the end users, including people who are homeless and those struggling with drug and alcohol addictions. The client also wanted to turn the business into something that's suitable for corporate retreats, where local businesses can offer a team-building session through an outdoor boot camp. Another audience is people who go to the gym but who might want to become members with Primal Roots as well as, or instead of, traditional gym sessions. So it was important to speak to quite a range of people, and the task was to understand what the pain points were with each group.

There's a certain amount of fear from the client viewpoint before a project begins, so we explain that the brief acts as a benchmark that says, "Okay, maybe

Clients will always know our typical approach is to create
two options. That will be explained in the proposal document,
and it also tends to come up in the initial chat.

there are things you won't like about the font or the color, but in terms of the broad principles of what the brand stands for, what it needs to say, and how it generally looks, we can tie that back to everything that's been established in the creative brief." If, for example, the CEO of the company doesn't like the color blue, that's irrelevant when considering whether it works for the objectives of the business.

The brief is essentially the structural framework to make sure that nothing goes wrong.

The brief is essentially the structural framework to make sure that nothing goes wrong in the creative interpretation that we share. When the content is agreed on, we typically go away for two or three weeks to develop the creative routes. Ninety percent of our clients leave the creative development stage entirely to us, but every now and again someone wants to see the initial thoughts before they're edited down.

Our clients know our typical approach is to create two options. That's explained in our proposal document and the initial chat. Other design firms might create three, four, five, or six options, but there are always two really good ones among them. We'd rather spend more time crafting those two than delivering six. You can undermine your credibility if you start to present more and more ideas because it should be quite clear how the work links back to the brief, so the more concentrated the ideas, the better they are.

A strategic approach

The amount of strategy involved depends on the job. We sometimes work on projects that are focused primarily on strategy and messaging and very little design. Other projects are more design-heavy and involve less strategy. We also have projects in which we might do a month of strategy before we even have an initial workshop around the design themes.

Because a lot of what we do is based on the messaging, attitude, character, and personality of the brand, one thing we try to deliver is a brand manifesto, kind of like a positioning statement. Clients often get one of these regardless of whether we work on strategy or creative efforts. It's a bit of a "spirit of the brand" document. For Primal Roots, the following manifesto was written to capture the essence and spirit of what they were as an organization. The headline was "Nature is Your Gym."

"The woods provide a natural alternative to every aspect of a traditional gym. Your gym floor is a bed of leaves. The cooling mist is your air conditioning. The dawn chorus provides your playlist. Leaves and trees breathe with you. Muddy paths mark your track. Animal instinct drives you forward. A wandering stream is your water fountain. And the setting sun sets your pace. This is nature's gym. This is Primal Roots."

The manifesto won't necessarily be shared

NATURE IS YOUR GYM

The woods provide a natural alternative
to every aspect of a traditional gym.

Your gym floor is a bed of leaves.
The cooling mist is your air conditioning.

The dawn chorus provides your playlist.
Leaves and trees breathe with you.

Muddy paths mark your track.
Animal instinct drives you forward.

A wandering stream, your water fountain.
The setting sun setting your pace.

This is nature's gym.
This is Primal Roots.

The brand manifesto won't necessarily be an external-facing
document, but it helps the client get into an emotional position
about what their brand stands for.

externally, but it helps get the client into an emotional position about what their brand stands for, what their messaging style is, and how they differ from their competitors. Capturing the attitude and spirit of the business is always a great jumping off point for the messaging we develop. We focus on the verbal first and then blend it with the visual as the project develops.

On finding ideas

Every project involves self-doubt, where you question your work over and over, which can be frustrating, but it means you eventually get to something that's appropriate for the client. You just have to work through it.

Having a break and leaving something for the day or working on a different project and coming back to it later, helps to crystallize an idea or distill things a little more. Sometimes getting out of the office or chatting things through with your client in more detail can free up your thinking and create space for additional ideas. Another direction is to consider the application in more detail—working back from where the design will be seen in context to the actual design idea rather than first crafting the idea and then working toward the application. Inverting your thought process is an attempt at getting your brain to fire in different ways.

Knowing when you've considered enough different options comes down to experience, and from making sure what you've developed delivers on every aspect of the brief. Design is about having that built-in ability to understand when something feels like it's an appropriate fit. There's an emotional part of that, but the functional side is the briefing document and making sure your work ticks those boxes.

We do our due diligence to ensure that any symbols we design don't infringe upon existing copyrights. It happens with brand naming, too—searching the Companies House database and trademark websites. Google images is helpful, but copyright is certainly an area that's becoming more difficult because when you're combining simple shapes and text, there's so much potential for there to be an overlap with something else.

The design presentation

We start with a recap of the brief and any outtakes from the workshop just to refresh everyone's memories, and then we'll lead the client on a journey through our two creative routes. Typically, it starts with us reading the manifesto statement and then we break it down—here's the identity, here's the messaging that sits alongside, here's your photographic style, and here's how they come together. We show everything from website homepages to advertising to social media mock-ups and sample tweets to the kinds of accompanying images, promoted Instagram posts, merchandise, and so on. What we show depends on the project scope.

To help reach consensus, we'll sometimes steer a client toward one of the two options. It depends on our feelings. Sometimes we have a favorite, and we let the client know. Sometimes we don't, or each route works in a slightly different way, where one idea focuses on more of a particular audience or a particular brand attitude, It's a case of saying, "Both of these work, and both address the brief, but do you feel that this one reflects you better than this one? Which are you more comfortable with?"

A presentation can be a lot for clients to take in when they've just seen the vision of what their

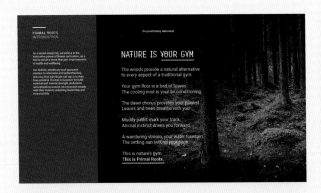
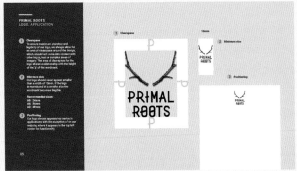

The guidelines focused on the logo, typography, tone of voice,
photographic style, and a wide range of sample applications.

business will look like. So after showing the two routes, we let the client have a discussion before we give our thoughts on a potential preference. It's easy to turn a room to think in one direction when you're the first person to speak. As much as we'd love to push them in our direction, we don't think it's appropriate at that point. They know the brand better than anyone so they need to have that gut reaction. Obviously, if there's silence or people aren't sure which one to go for, we'll then say, "Okay, these are our thoughts, and this is why." But it's helpful to let the client speak first.

When the client picks one of the two options, we listen to feedback and usually refine that route once or twice. The purpose of this phase isn't for the client to ask for a new route. If we received that kind of feedback, it'd feel like the brief was wrong in the first place. Client opinion is usually split between the two presented ideas, but for Primal Roots, the decision was unanimous.

Developing guidelines

After the chosen route has been refined, we move onto the guidelines phase. We always say to clients that the guidelines are there for two reasons— consistency and creativity. Consistency is about showing the core toolkit elements, such as the logo, color codes, fonts, the tone of voice, and the creative headlines, whereas creativity is about showing how those elements come together, how they're used. Guidelines will help clients whether they're producing something in-house or they're working with other agencies—which is often the case.

Some of our more established clients have told us their existing guidelines only show where the logo is positioned on marketing collateral, the

necessary clear space around it, color values, and the accompanying font name. There's nothing in terms of implementation. One of the best ways to prepare guidelines is to show as many best-practice contextual applications as possible. Then things are much less likely to go astray when our work is implemented because the client can see what their advertising can look like, how their social media profiles and messages can appear, and so on.

The guidelines are there for two reasons— consistency and creativity.

Sometimes we'll work as a partner or guardian over the brand, where the client sends us items that other people produce, and we'll give our feedback before the client approves with the third party. Sometimes we'll just keep an eye on clients' social media to see what they're producing, and if anything isn't quite right, we'll get in touch and say we're happy to provide additional guidance to help things stay on track. Clients are glad of the help. Sometimes it's things they maybe can't see because of their internal processes, or the time frames they're working to, and it's good to have a fresh pair of eyes on things.

PRIMAL ROOTS

"This is nature's gym. This is Primal Roots."

To summarize, guidelines aren't rules, they should allow creativity.

Studio marketing

We launched with our founder, Ryan Tym, working on his own from his spare bedroom. There was the foundation of one client, as well as investment based on a five-year-plan. Three investors gave an additional safety net in terms of cash flow and business growth. You don't often hear about design firms starting in that way, but with a sense of risk aversion, we wanted to make sure there was as much structure in place as possible. Sometimes people might freelance their way into becoming an agency. That wasn't for us because it can be quite easy to end up doing projects for other agencies where you get comfortable doing work that other people find, rather than focusing solely on your own brand.

We're now based in one of the WeWork coworking spaces in a building of private offices with a shared kitchen and a member network of 40,000 or 50,000 businesses around the world. In the first year, the work we picked up through the network brought in more than we were paying in rent, so being there made sense. The more people you surround yourself with, the greater the chance that one of those people will know someone who needs design or branding work. It's amazing how somebody who you might've randomly chatted to three years ago might say, "Oh by the way, I've put you in touch with these guys."

There's also a holistic thing in having a strong online presence. We get many cold inquiries through our website, including a recent one from someone who read one of our thought leadership articles.

Keep an eye on social media for potential projects, and the government tender database is always filled with work that's available for designers and branding agencies. Doing talks at relevant events can also build awareness of your brand.

There isn't one brilliant way of marketing yourself; instead, it involves doing as many of these things as possible to keep raising your profile.

Key points

When starting a project, you need to get an understanding of your client's business, their ambitions, and the key deliverables.

Never begin any creative work until receiving at least partial payment.

Working with those who are prepared to take their brand in a brave direction can make your work a lot more interesting.

Don't neglect the verbal side of the identity, because it's just as important as the visual side.

Leaving your work for a day and sleeping on it can help to clarify thoughts on a particular design route.

It helps to recap the brief at the beginning of your design presentation.

Presenting too many ideas can undermine your credibility.

Remember that the client knows their brand better than anyone.

Don't think of guidelines as rules. Craft them to give the client scope to be creative.

TRAGÖDIE
+

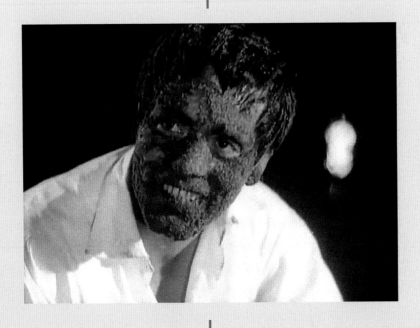

+
PASOLINI

Base

Brussels + Geneva + New York
www.basedesign.com

Project: Ruhrtriennale

Music, dance, theater, performance, and fine arts in the former industrial buildings of the Ruhr Area—that's the Ruhrtriennale.

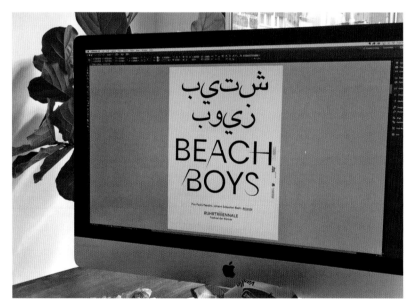

Right at the start of the project we proposed something that we never had with any other client—to design everything together.

A new artistic director takes the helm of the festival every three years. In our case, Dutch director Johan Simons headed the events. His main focus, in which he has a lot of experience, was getting audiences to see things that were otherwise difficult to see. For example, he has tried many ways throughout his career to make opera more accessible and to bring it to a wider audience. Johan's approach here was also about accessibility.

Rules of client acquisition

We have three rules that help us to decide which projects to take on. First, we won't accept a job if we don't have access to the decision maker. It sounds obvious, but it's vital because without that access you end up talking to people who say, "Okay, I'll ask my boss," and that leads to delays and other problems.

Second, we set our entry fee at €50,000 ($58,000). It's a lot of money, but anything below it is too small for our structure. From day one, on any project, at least three people are immediately engaged in the work.

Third is the question of cultural fit. It's up to our partners and business developers to say, "Okay, I feel like this is the right person for us to work with" or "I don't feel like it for x, y, z reason." For example, if a potential client's only motivation is profit or more income, then we'd probably decline the project, because we'll never have that cultural fit. Our main focus is with the quality of the relationship and the project outcome.

When any of our team has a lead for a new client, we write what we call "a vision brief." It's a one-page internal document that explains why the project is interesting, why we should accept it, and whether it complies with our criteria.

If, as in one of the criteria, a €50,000 ($58,000) job is actually €30,000 ($35,000), but the partner or business developer really thinks we should take it, he or she has to give the reason why the company should be on board. Any project acceptance needs unanimity, and we go through these reviews every Monday.

If a potential client's only motivation is profit, or more income, then we'd probably decline.

Project deliverables

Our task was to create the Ruhrtriennale global concept and identity, including poster templates and digital and print guidelines. The client had a digital agency to develop the website and an internal team to produce a tremendous amount of collateral, such as bags and promotional items, so a lot of the follow-up

The typeface was the star of the show, the leading lady,
with character, elegance, and dynamism.

implementation was done on the client side.

It was still a big project for us, involving a lot of work. It was certainly not our most profitable one, but there's always a balance we need to reach in the studio between profit, visibility, and excitement.

How we price

This project was special because our interest in the brief resulted in us spending more time on it than we should have. We generally price our work by gathering the designers, writers, and strategists to evaluate how much time each project phase will take, whether it's five days, two weeks, a month, and so on. We also take into account the size of the client and the potential reach—you don't charge a local client the same amount as a client with international visibility.

In our initial client meetings, we discuss the scope of work and the expectations. When the client has a clear idea about what they think is needed, then we can ask about their budget. It's important that we get an initial idea so we know approximately what resources we can allocate and include in the proposal. So from the earliest discussions, we're thinking of how many people we'll need and how many days for each, and we then arrive at a proposal that meets what the client can invest. The budget also serves as a framework for us. When we start a project, we know we can spend eight or ten days, or two or three weeks on the first phase, and we know the time frame for completing a first presentation.

It took us many years to learn to do that properly. The alternative is that rather than us being in control of our work, the client and external forces lead the project, and that's not what we want. Our goal is to

work in full autonomy. Always.

We often slice the proposal into different phases as our pricing is linked to the resources of people and time and our objective is for the client to remain autonomous. So if, after phase one, the client thanks us, accepts our fee, but doesn't want to continue for a particular reason, we're okay with that. He or she doesn't have to sign up for everything. It's important that trust is built through the various project phases, and although it almost never happens, the client can leave at any point. Our goal is to objectivize each phase of the process and make sure the client is always aware of our added value as designers and partners.

We normally invoice per phase, but it depends. If we have a project that totals around €250,000 ($292,000), similar to the website we finished for the Foundation Cartier in Paris, we would agree to invoice at the end of each month for one year, almost like a retainer.

We accept payment by bank transfer, and in our European studios, we try to keep all finances in euros. With one of our Middle Eastern clients, we prepared our price in euros, which they agreed to before telling us it was all right to bill them in dollars, trying to bargain a little. We declined and then reiterated that we request payment in euros. Every client has a different cultural background so it's important to understand that and to be able to adapt.

Negotiating

There's an element of negotiation with almost every job. Our policy is that if you send a quote for €50,000 ($58,000), and the client comes back and says, "No, €30,000 [$35,000]," then you're starting on the wrong

DRONE
+

+
METAL

The colors were predominantely duotone to maximize impact.

foot because you're negotiating the exact same work for less money. We don't do that. Instead we'll remove some of the deliverables because otherwise the client will think, "Okay, I got it for €30,000 [$35,000], but why not €25,000 [$29,000]?" It becomes an endless discussion. We also negotiate with one thing in mind: We need to be paid for the added value we bring, for what we do well. With Ruhrtriennale, we could have delivered so many more items, but we didn't fight to do it. We don't want to overextend ourselves just to be able to send one more invoice. It's about finding a balance that works for you.

Successful negotiation was addressing the needs of the client while retaining our excitement for the task.

The client asked for a lot, and when we sent our quote, they told us they only had half that amount. Successful negotiation was addressing the needs of the client while retaining our excitement for the task.

That was probably the trickiest thing for us in this case—reaching that point where we'd say, "No, you have to do this on your side because it's not in the contract." We don't work for free.

The contract

Many people see the contract linked only to money, but a good contract is much more than that. It's an agreement between two people or two companies that also covers the deliverables, the time frame, and the methodology, including the people assigned to the project. The more precise the contract language, the better, because it helps avoid misinterpretation about what you're going to do and the items you're going to deliver. You invite problems if these things aren't carefully specified.

The client either needs to sign and return the contract document or express agreement by email. We then immediately invoice for an advance payment of 30 percent. That up-front fee is to ensure a commitment on both sides to the way the project is going to proceed. In our New York studio, the advance payment is 50 percent because it's more difficult to get a commitment in New York than it is in Brussels or Geneva. In New York, there's so much competition and so many good studios. It's a very aggressive environment. Even if people sign the contract and agree to collaborate, they may leave you after a month for reasons you can't always control. Of course, we have great clients in New York, but sometimes it's particularly tough. There's this idea in the United States that, "I pay you, so you do what I want," but most of the time clients don't actually know what they want. Also, when our New York team finishes the job, the client will often move on. Whereas in Brussels

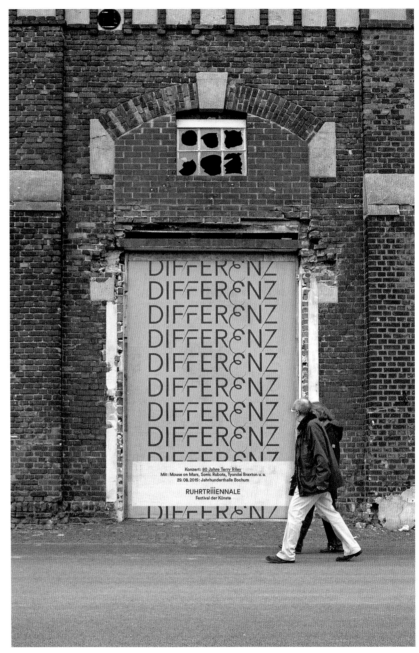

The map is the icon of the triennale, bringing everything together: the region, the people, the program.

or Geneva, we maintain longer client relationships, sometimes for eight, nine, or ten years. Building a trusting, long-term relationship is possible in our New York studio—one wonderful client has been with us for seventeen years—but it's much more difficult to achieve. There's a cultural difference where, almost every time, they'll approach other studios, placing you in competition.

It's key to get a signed contract before starting.

We've been in business for more than twenty years, so we've made every possible mistake. One of the things we've learned is that it's key to get a signed contract before we start a project. We also avoid having one person discuss the price as well as do the design work. Although most designers need to do this, because they're working for their own studio, the problem is that you're caught in the position where you have to work with the client while also be the bad cop over contracts and money. When you separate the two, it's much easier because the client immediately understands who will design and who will ensure adherence to the deadlines and the budget. Clients like to know who's doing what, so if we happen to encounter temporary financial issues, they don't automatically jeopardize the design.

Problems arise if you leave room for the client

to think that a specific deliverable could be this, or it could be that, and sometimes you'll be left shortchanged. Clients are clever, they can pick up on contract flaws. We love our clients in the Middle East not only because they're great people but also very astute when it comes to contracts and negotiations. They can take a lot more of your time and energy than you initially expected because your contract lacks precision. Your clients will respect you for being tough about the specifics, but if you're too relaxed and uncertain, they can keep asking for things and you can't do anything about it because they're right— you weren't precise enough.

When any issues occur during a project, no matter where your clients are located, people will always return to the original contract, so it better be detailed and thorough.

Understanding the client
Including the client in our thought process is vital, which is why the first phase of a project is generally a client workshop. The phases in our estimates can be customized to each client, but that initial, inclusive workshop is crucial. Most of the time the client will implement their new identity themselves because they need to be autonomous; they are the project, so we see our work as facilitating their path to autonomy. It's their brand, their festival, their Ruhrtriennale. We will help them, we will provide tools and ideas, but we will not do everything for them. It's important that they know that from day one. We often remind clients, "It's not our brand. It's yours."

How we worked with the client on the festival was especially interesting, because instead of the client briefing us with, "We have this show, with this

ABEND-
LAND
+
+
MORGEN-
LAND

If you put a poster in the street that shows Beethoven or Mozart
a lot of people will automatically say it's not for them.

director, this is the content, these are our objectives, we want this, and we want that," the first page of Johan Simons' brief was a short story. "A father is driving his son along a busy highway in the Ruhr area and suddenly there's a huge billboard with just one line of text: 'Be embraced.' The kid asks his father what it means, and the father answers, 'I don't know.'" That was it. That was the brief. We thought it was wonderfully exciting.

Johan had quite a straightforward vision for everything—not only the content of the show and the creators, musicians, directors, and others whom he wanted to invite, but also with the communication. The main idea was this thought "Be embraced." The text in German means a little more than the English translation. It refers to a physical, welcoming attitude, treating people in a benevolent way. Johan said this is what he wanted to do during his three years as director.

Conducting research

In our studio, we have three people dedicated to research, strategy, and writing. We don't treat our projects as some form of production line where we first do the research, then the strategy, and then hand things to a designer. That's a weak working method. We always work in a collaborative way. We always collaborate in an iterative way. As soon as we had the Ruhrtriennale brief, we gathered a team of two or three designers, one writer, and one strategist and we put them in what we call a "war room" for nine or ten days. We do this a lot so they can work together in the same environment. The team covers the room with images, references, mood boards, ideas, texts, whatever. Someone from digital always attends those meetings, which is a "must-have" in today's

communication world. It is also crucial that everyone learns from everyone else.

As part of our research, we visited various venues around the Ruhr region. It's an industrial area, between cities and countryside, where huge production plants had been abandoned but have since been refurbished into event venues. The region is culturally diverse, with many workers from Turkey, Iraq, and various other countries. Johan was organizing this high-quality opera, dance, and theater event in this typically blue-collar area, and the challenge was to get close to people who would otherwise never go to an opera. Johan said that if you put a poster in the street that shows Beethoven or Mozart, many people will automatically say it's not for them. We needed to embrace a whole region through the mediums of opera, theater, and contemporary dance. It was exciting because it was extremely ambitious.

The role of the strategist

Strategy isn't separate from other parts of a project. It's there to frame and give voice to your creative work. It's the collaborative work of the strategist and designer, and we research and design within that conceptual frame. Words are extremely important in our design process at Base. Younger designers often don't think words and writing are important. In our studio, we ask all designers to write. They need to prepare their concepts in writing as well as images, playing with words in the same way they play with type, imagery, and color. That's why one of the keys of the Ruhrtriennale solution was to combine words and imagery.

We have three copywriters in our team, but just because you're a copywriter doesn't mean you

The underlying identity system was so simple that we felt
comfortable designing posters with the client.

can't bring images to the table in the same way that designers can bring text. It's important to do more than what is on your business card. Of course, people have specific roles and specialties, but our copywriters can create excellent (and different) mood boards in the same way that our designers can write and bring other kinds of input in words.

One of the main flaws with younger designers is that they don't think words and writing are important to them.

The idea

A sketch was made in one of our brainstorming sessions that read, "we + you = us." We put it at the beginning of our presentation and the client said it was exactly the message and attitude they wanted to convey across the entire festival and communications. So their project challenge was met with this idea

of "addition"—combining an addition symbol with various images to evoke feelings or prompt questions from those we needed to reach. The tools were simple: pairing the selected images with the bespoke typeface, so once the idea was in place, it was relatively straightforward to create a variety of outcomes. The objective was to free ourselves from the usual concert visuals, in which composers such as Mozart or Beethoven were promoted with high-level conceptual images. That would scare people away and contradict Johan's vision. We began by thinking of the content we'd use for each piece. What makes it attractive? Why should you look at it? Each piece wasn't necessarily formed by thinking of music. It could be something crazy or just something of interest. We gave ourselves total freedom with no imagery guidelines. Instead, the content was the driving force.

We worked with Johan throughout the three years of his directorship. The first year was very time consuming as we had to define every element of the identity, but much less work was needed during the following two years as they simply involved thinking a little more about the concept and adapting the brand colors.

At the start of the project, we proposed something that we had never done with any other client—that we design everything together. It was a gamble, but we felt confident enough that with the level of understanding, freedom, and fun we had between us, it was the right way to go. It was also something that could only be achieved because the "addition" system was so simple and enjoyable to play with.

We held annual workshops in Brussels or the Ruhr region, where the client would share details on what made each show unique—the stories, the artists,

In one of the workshops the client suggested putting posters on the ground—something we would never have thought of.

or the composers. Each session involved five people from the client side and three or four from ours. As an example, the client would say, "This is the production for Pasolini, this is the content, it's about workers in the south of Italy," and so on, and then everyone from both teams would throw ideas around, search online for images, pair them with text in the brand typeface, and try things out on a large screen. After half an hour, we'd finish one of the posters. We had never designed with the client at our side, but it was so much fun, and it allowed us to create about eighteen posters in a day. The conversation about each was so enriching, and also gave the client ideas on how to explain their events to the press.

This workshop gave us a full day of understanding how a production like this is done. The things we learned were tremendous. In turn, the client would learn how we'd translate their events into a visual identity. It was total freedom on the choice of images. In one, we'd show a black and white photo from a famous photographer, for another, it'd be a Space Invader icon, and for another, we'd opt for a type-only approach. The distinctive typeface and color code would tie everything together and ensure global consistency. The process was completely open, which brought a lot of energy to the communication, taking opera from a place that was very conservative to one that was contemporary, daring, and exciting.

The theme for the second year was "Liberty, Equality, Fraternity." It was political, about the migrant problem in Europe and specifically Germany because Johan wanted to address that. We produced a huge street poster with a green background that simply showed the word "freedom." People wondered what it was about, and as they continued to see it, they'd make their own connection. We weren't giving

answers. Only questions. That's what made it exciting for both us and the audience.

The client suggested putting posters on the ground in the area's main train station. We would never have thought of that. As some of the images offended certain people, there was a debate in the local newspaper about the content, raising the profile of the event.

When we conduct a workshop, we need to be in the same room as the client, to breathe the same air, and to eat the same sandwiches. Video conferencing, with two or three people, is okay to exchange thoughts, but we prefer working in person. We once conducted a workshop with a client in Beirut, which was very fruitful. In addition, we got to spend four days in Beirut, which is an amazing city, so why do it any other way?

It's for you to decide when the work is finished.

When to stop experimenting

You decide when the work is finished. If there's a deadline, of course you need to be ready on time, so each of our projects has a leader—a designer, a partner, or someone else, depending on the project. When we research ideas and directions together, at some point the leader needs to summarize things: "This is probably the way to go, do you agree? Is this what we want to proceed with?" Everyone needs to

POESIE
+
+
WUT-
MANAGEMENT
+

Poetry + anger management

be in agreement, and if someone in the room doesn't like the direction for a specific reason, we need to do more research.

These sessions can often be difficult and tiring. For example, a project team had been working intensely for three days before one of our partners arrived and said, "I don't think we have anything yet." It wasn't easy for him to say that, but at the same time, being demanding of each other is essential. There's a lot of discussion, contradiction, and debate, but it's healthy. We once made the mistake of knowing the result wasn't the best we could do, and it came back to bite us with a dissatisfied client. So it's better if someone just says, "No, we're not there yet."

Honesty

When you can say to the person working next to you that you don't like or understand what they created or that it needs more work, you've reached a level of honesty that's key. We accept that if the design isn't there, it's not there, and we need to get back to the table.

It's a long process to reach this stage, but it's linked to everything we do in our company. It has to do with commitment and freedom of speech. When we started our studio, we didn't have any management skills because in design school you don't learn how to manage people, how to talk to them, gather them, lead them. You're taught how to use typefaces and color, but you don't know how to behave as an entrepreneur or a leader. Because of that, we soon reached a point where the outside world was deciding how we would work. The client would say, "I need this by Thursday," and we'd be under great pressure with deadlines. So we wanted to recover our autonomy as well as build a strong internal culture.

What we have now is pretty simple. All the people at Base are completely autonomous —they are their own project leaders. They can work at the studio, from home, arrive early, and leave early. They commit to what they create and they're in charge of what they produce. To keep things on track, we have four mandatory meetings each week. The first is on Monday morning, where we all gather in the central room for half an hour. We each fill a sticky note with our personal challenges for the week. It can be, "I want to leave by 5 p.m. every day for sports" or "I need to finish this presentation by Thursday." They're your personal challenges. You pin them on the wall and explain them to the team. It's a commitment to yourself and to your teammates.

Wednesday morning's creative meeting is crucial. The whole team has to be there. It's the same in the Brussels, New York, or Geneva Base studios, so if people move among studios, they can keep up with what's happening. The meeting is led by different people and starts with what we call "inclusions"— a system that helps each person reach honesty. You answer four questions: How do I feel today? What has happened to me since last time? What will I bring to this meeting? What do I expect? So when people aren't in good shape, they have to say so. For example, "I fought with my girlfriend last night and I'm not in a good mood. I didn't want to come in today." That's how honesty gets triggered and, amazingly, it also prompts empathy. Our team wants to help those who aren't doing so well. If we feel that someone on the team has low energy, we can see that immediately and offer to help with whatever project they're working on.

After the inclusions, we have what we call "models," in which you tell everyone what you're

Be embraced.

working on and you ask the right people whether they can help you for an hour or two. It gives you fresh eyes and new input on your project.

On Thursday, we gather together for lunch. We each take turns to cook for the entire studio. It's not about work—it's about generosity. You can cook, or you can buy food, but you're responsible for feeding the group that day.

Finally, on Friday, we go back to the challenges from Monday and check on the successes and failures. If you succeed, obviously you had a great week. If you failed, you explain why, so at least you learn, and the team learns with you.

The system can work just as well for a studio of three people as it can with a larger company. Sometimes we use this inclusion process in client workshops to reach a high level of honesty. It's a brilliant tool.

Presenting ideas

If we have a client workshop session, we will at least agree on the objectives and the framework in which we play with design and words. This is essentially a first phase. We love keeping this phase together with the design, rather than separating the two because it's difficult to explain what you're going to do without showing it. We strongly believe in trying to convince by doing, so we often present only one option—not because it's the only one, but because it is our answer, the one we believe in. In that initial presentation, we communicate the strategy, integrated with words and design.

We don't want to sound pretentious, but we're rarely off when we present a particular direction. This is because we've spent so much time building a relationship with the client. Sometimes disagreement arises over personal preferences or tastes, e.g., the client might not like a particular typeface. They soon realize that these are details of taste, so our response is, "Okay, but does it feel wrong?"

Very early in our projects, we tell the client how the objective with feedback is to avoid, "I like it" or "I don't like it," and instead ask, "Is it the right answer? Is it what I need in terms of my objectives?" If a client thinks along the lines of whether they like or don't like it, then they'll soon ask, "Can you move this here, that there?" Then you've become a producer, and the client is designing. So if we hear, "I don't really like this," then we're very straightforward in explaining, "You need to be very precise about what you don't like, and why, because we can, and will, correct it, but we'll not correct it twenty times until you tell us, 'Actually, I don't know what I want.'"

What's interesting is how you can prevent this by asking the client, "Can you show us something that you're really fond of, something that impresses you in the same area of work or in different sectors?" Then we get references to help us shape the visual environment the client wants to see or is at ease with.

Trademarking and guidelines

Trademarking a logo is a necessary evil in today's world. It's very strict, very expensive, and very basic at the same time. It's not our work. It's the work of a lawyer. (We have one we commission when we need to trademark something.)

Of course, we need to be aware of trademarks because they can influence what we create. The branding business is changing so fast that the relationship with time is now one of our main concerns. For example, up until a few years ago we would design guidelines and print a detailed guideline

The palette was changed for the second year,
while the same underlying system was retained.

document. We now advise against that because it takes so much time that when the guidelines are finished, they're almost obsolete. Instead, we simplify the process by designing what we call a toolbox. It includes the basic tools used to identify a brand: not only the graphics, but the wording, tone of voice, social media communication, and every dimension, but in a very simple way, creating a simple tool that's easy to use. Nobody wants to read a 100-page manual.

The branding business is changing so fast that the relationship with time is now one of our main conerns.

A big part of our work is to break the fear of the client. It's okay to fail, but it's not okay to do nothing because you're afraid to fail. The worst brands are too scared to try new things. So after the client takes the toolbox and tests it in real life, we correct what doesn't work and continue with what does, getting into a dynamic of change. We've pushed this working process tremendously in the past few years.

Measuring success

Most of the time, clients don't know what constitutes a successful project, which is crazy in a way because they spend a lot of money without truly thinking of the desired outcome. Though we didn't have specific metrics for Ruhrtriennale, the clients were extremely happy for a couple of reasons: They generated a huge amount of publicity, exceeded the planned number of ticket sales, and also created debate within the local community and press. They considered it a success, as did we.

We have surveyed our main clients, and one of the key markers of success was that they felt stronger internally, both as a brand and as a company, by identifying what makes them unique or different. So the result isn't solely based on external communication. It's also internal, helping the client to be more unified behind a vision and direction. That's of significant value.

Advice for working with clients

First, it comes down to the quality of how you listen. Younger designers will sometimes focus on what they initially want to do with the brief, but the listening phase is extremely important. More than that, it's crucial. You fully address the client's issue by adapting and by bringing your expertise to their brief.

Second, dare to challenge the various processes if they don't suit you. Our client was in Germany and we were in Belgium, which wasn't straightforward, but we organized collaborative sessions to work together. The fact that you're around the same table for one or two days, eating and drinking together, makes it much more interesting, and the key to any good job is a good

Event road signage

human relationship. Some younger designers don't appreciate that, and tend to stay at home or in their studio, alone, on their computer. That's not good. That's part of the problem. They need to be with their clients, and to understand them. Building these relationships is one of the nicest parts of being a designer.

The key to any good job is a good human relationship. Some younger designers don't appreciate that.

Third, be demanding of yourself and the client. If there's something you don't understand or like or feel uncomfortable with, ask about it or challenge it. It's okay to disagree on things.

Fourth, think about how to prompt, "Oh, I didn't expect that, wow." Surprise is the best gift you can give to anyone, especially your client—bringing something that was unexpected to the table. A surprise could be, "Okay, will you come to Brussels and we will do this together?" That was one of the best ideas we had during this process.

Key points

Always ensure that you have access to the decision maker on every project.

When your client has a clear idea about what they need, ask how much they're willing to spend.

To set your price, evaluate the time you'll need for each phase of the work.

Your client doesn't initially need to invest in everything from your proposal. Trust can be built as the project progresses, with more work added later.

Never negotiate the same amount of work for less money. Instead, remove some of the deliverables.

Requesting advance payment ensures commitment on both sides.

If problems arise, people will always return to the original contract. Make sure it's thorough and clarifies expectations.

Including the client in your thought process is vital.

Don't separate strategy from design. Merge them to craft a compelling outcome.

After a presentation, if a client tells you he or she doesn't like the design, reply by asking, "But does it feel right?" It can also help you to make the right changes or refinements when you ask to see visual references of things your client likes in the same sector.

The worst clients are scared to try new things, but you can help and guide them to overcome their fear.

A successful identity project needs internal buy-in, where the client feels more unified behind a vision and direction. It's then much easier for the client to communicate that vision externally.

While you should always be demanding of yourself, it is equally important to be demanding of your client.

Pharus

São Paulo
www.pharusdesign.com

Project: Rio Cello

Rio Cello is a classical music event that invades the streets of Rio de Janeiro with art, music, and dance. The music repertoire promotes the encounter between classical and popular, with concerts of contemporary cello, choro, jazz, tango, and rock music.

One of the main guiding questions we asked ourselves was,
"How can we turn the sound of music into something
palpable and visual?"

Rio Cello was created in 1994 by David Chew, a prominent English cellist living in Brazil, as a means of honoring Brazilian composer Heitor Villa-Lobos, and bringing classical music to a wider audience.

David's aim is to connect musicians from around the world with the local population, for free. This was a beautiful project that deserved our best work. Our design coordinator in Rio knew David personally. She admired the cultural and social outlook of the event and saw the creative potential of the project in energizing the Pharus team. As such, she offered to develop the entire visual identity for the 2017 Rio Cello on a pro bono basis, inaugurating a creative partnership that has been extended beyond that year.

The brief
We're usually provided with a project brief to help us prepare our proposal, but most of the information comes from discussions with the client. Lately we've noticed a decreasing quality in client briefs, finding them empty with differentiation and lacking expectations and success criteria. These details are vital to avoid basing the analysis on simplistic likes and dislikes. Rather than personal preferences, strong design should focus on what is appropriate. We like to challenge the outlook of brands, and we always show creative paths that can change the market, but we understand that not every brand wants this kind of change, so we need to agree on this at the beginning.

There's great importance in design planning, where we map the present, in terms of competitors and benchmarks, and the future, in terms of trends and new aesthetic approaches. We request access to all brand assets, and we ask what current and potential market sectors the client might operate in.

Project deliverables
Printed material ranged from posters, banners, and identification badges, to the event schedule and DVD inlay cards. Other promotional items included T-shirts, eco bags, bookmarks, Scotch tape, and Havaianas sandals. On the digital side was an event video to greet musicians as they arrived at Rio's Galeão International Airport. Bach was the soundtrack. We spread event images across social networks, developed the website, and created a video poster for digital billboards. Across the various venues, at the opening of each show, the chant of a cello could be heard while a graphic form danced to its rhythm.

Designers have an environmental responsibility that's greater than most professions.

We always try to create something with a reduced amount of plastic or we recommend paper without glossy or special finishes because designers have an environmental responsibility that's greater than most professions, so we must do our best to encourage green thinking.

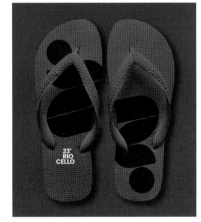

We presented our client with three creative paths. Here are
a couple of applications from the two that were unused.

Terms and conditions

Simply put, our terms and conditions (T&C) cover the deliverables, the number of potential rounds of modifications and people decided to the job, the project time frame, payment conditions, and cancellation terms.

We request agreement by email. It's essential that we have our T&C in order to protect the agency because most projects involve referring the client back to certain points in the original document. We work with intangible items that can be open to interpretation, to likes and dislikes. Being clear in the terms makes it much easier to negotiate when, for example, a project may need an additional month of work. There are many ways to negotiate during the course of a project, but only when you've clearly defined the original scope.

Certain clients will have their own terms of engagement that we need to sign, and others will sometimes query our terms before a project begins. Queries are good because it means the terms have been read. Client uncertainty is usually about the limited rounds of modification or the time frame. We've needed to prepare a detailed schedule to prove it's possible to deliver in the stipulated time.

Fortunately for us, we've never had to pursue legal help as a result of a project going wrong. We're sure that's partly because of having our clients agree to our working terms.

Knowing what to charge

Our fees grant the client an exclusive team for a set period of time. We base our pricing on what the market has determined for similar agencies, the number of people we devote to the task, how many hours the team will need, the number of creative paths we'll present, and how large the client is. There's always flexibility to change or add smaller deliverables. Sometimes, as with the Rio Cello project, we exchanged our time for the greater good.

How we invoice our clients mostly depends on the total amount. We generally request 100 percent in advance for small budgets, 60 percent for medium, and 30 percent for large. Or we sometimes accept payment that reflects more of a retainer, where a monthly fee is agreed from the outset.

We increase our pricing across the board on an annual basis, at least adjusting for inflation. However, if we notice that we're spending more and more time on a retainer project and it starts to demand more people, we'll raise the price. When it comes to negotiating with clients, one of our teachers taught the lesson that you need to have two baskets: one holds the things you don't give up, and the other holds what's open to negotiation.

Estimating the project time frame

Throughout the years, we have learned the time we usually take to complete each stage of a project. Knowing the team and understanding the internal processes make it easier to prepare estimates. We've established a minimum time frame to guarantee completion of essential creative stages, but it varies according to the project complexity. Perhaps due to the culture of advertising, it's common in the design profession that clients expect fast returns. After all, customers are often the same across both areas. There'll also be projects where a delivery deadline is set in stone right from the briefing stage because of product launches, for example. So we're always open

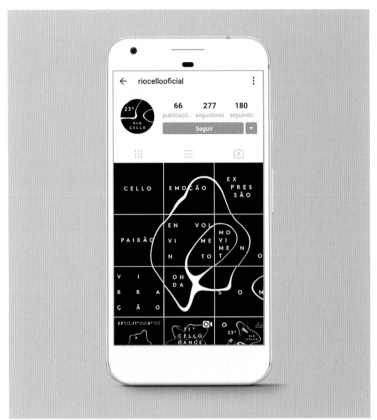

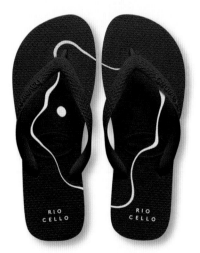

The promotional items we produced ranged from banners and
ID badges, to Scotch tape and Havaianas sandals.

to working to time frames determined by the client. In such cases, the time we devote to developing the strategy also changes. You can't have a one-month work attitude if the delivery is in a week.

We face the problem the same way regardless of what we earn. This is why it's important not to undersell your skills. If a client wants you to work for less than you normally would and spend the same amount of time on the project as you normally would, that can easily lead to heightened stress and a strain on schedules.

The Rio Cello project is one that had a pre-established deadline: the event opening day.

We created a retroactive time line, taking into account the approval time of the event's supporters and sponsors and the production of the design elements—some needed to be ready one month before the event, with the remainder due by launch day. From the date of the briefing, we allocated one month for the development of three different creative paths, and another month to finalize the artwork and have individual pieces ready for use.

The pro bono relationship

Creative partnerships for pro bono design differ from those in more typical commercial work. Each party offers its specialized services for the better of the project, complementing each other through mutual interest, rather than the agreed upon price. Thus, the contracted-contractor dynamics fall away, the exchange becomes more open, and the client's trust in our expertise ensures the work is more likely to surprise from the creative point of view. For the Rio Cello project, we had the freedom to conduct it in the way we considered most applicable, exploring fields

not yet visited, proposing specific creation processes, and trying new possibilities. This was a dream for any creator—and any partner.

Conducting research

We believe in aesthetics with meaning, in a design that connects beauty and strategy, turning the intangible into reality. Each project lets us use our curiosity to increase our knowledge and improve our visual repertoire. Going far beyond visual and verbal audits, we connect unlikely subjects through investigating the universe of the project. With each new job, we embrace experts in outside fields so we can work toward becoming experts ourselves.

It's important not to undersell your skills.

For Rio Cello, all the Pharus designers were involved in brainstorming and creative workshops. We invited a music teacher and luthier to deepen our discussions. It was important to immerse ourselves in classical music. We went to concerts by the Brazilian Symphony Orchestra, of which event founder David Chew is one of the main cellists. We interviewed David, other musicians, as well as music teachers. We participated in a lecture on creativity in which David, as a guest, musically expressed his passions

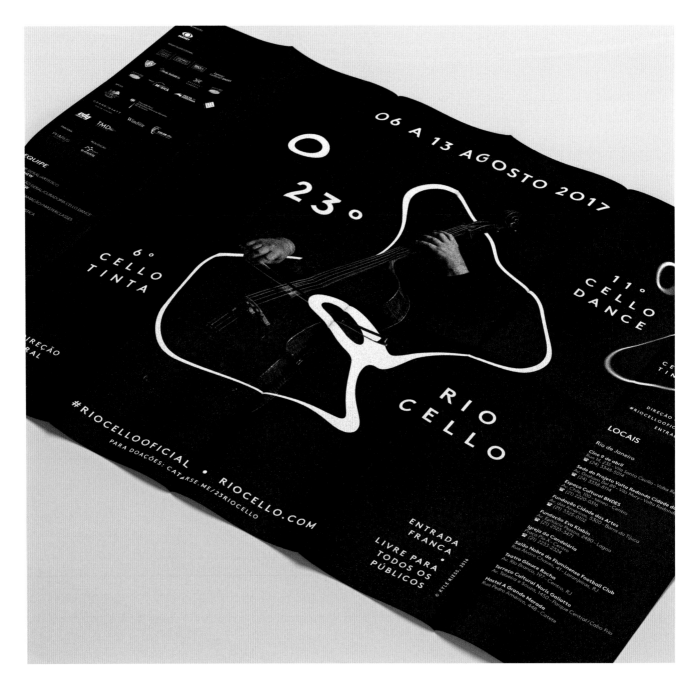

Event schedule

and influences and spoke of his motivations behind the event creation. We made endless playlists so we could feel the music in our veins, and we observed the body movement of cellists embracing their cellos as if they were one entity—the drawing of the moving bow and the reverberations of the notes vibrating in the belly. All this heightened our experience and understanding of the music.

We researched all the past Rio Cellos, as well as other music events around the world—if only to distance ourselves from their solutions. We do extensive research on other solutions that have been developed so that if we find something very similar, we change routes immediately.

We visited exhibitions in museums and galleries in Rio and São Paulo, and went to the Venice Biennale. We looked at the design and construction of the instrument and the materials and finishings used. We dug deep into secondhand bookstores, searching musical textbooks for scores and symbols that would let us recognize and understand music's visual codes. We discovered a world of sound science with analogical experiments that generated images from vibrations. All this was just a start, and of course we couldn't forget the city that lends its name to the event.

One of the main guiding questions we asked ourselves was, "How can we turn the sound of music into something palpable and visual?" To help with the answer, we conducted an exercise in which we'd listen to the cello and attempt to translate what we heard into form, color, material, and texture. For the exercise, we selected eleven cello pieces according to the event theme and history. Among other compositions, the playlist included Cello Suite

no. 1 in G major by J. S. Bach, Bachianas Brasileiras by Heitor Villa-Lobos, and various cello renditions from movie soundtracks. We wanted to create visual manifestations that would result in a diversity of form, colors, and sensations.

On experimentation

We believe in freedom to experience. Experiencing and experimenting is to make room for the unexpected. It's about opening possibilities that your imagination could not foresee because they come from the action itself. It's necessary to record many alternative directions and then take a break, analyze, and grasp the best ideas. We never create just one idea. If our first idea is indeed the best outcome, that's only because it stood out among so many others that we later explored. Fundamental to innovation is the experience of experimenting.

The process for Rio Cello was developed exclusively for the brief, where we tried to give shape to sound through its own vibration. We set up an apparatus consisting of a sound box, can, ball, mirror, and laser pen. When paired with the sound of the cello, the ball vibrates and the mirror that projects the laser moves. It generated a constantly mutating drawing that follows the nuances of sound. The result was the main idea for the identity.

But what form should we use? What song? The circular shape was born of the geometry of the instrument, while the song was an excerpt from the prelude to Bach's Cello Suite no. 1 in G major—easily recognizable in a project that seeks to unite classical with popular. The digitized result came from testing

Event posters, teaser posters, and eco-bags

a variety of responsive codes in video editing software. Digital work tools are common to every designer. What makes the difference is how we use them. Despite shifts to digital, what we cannot do is leave out the three main tools of any creative activity, which are, as the physicist Richard Feynman liked to say, a pencil, paper, and a trash can.

The three main tools of any creative activity are a pencil, paper, and a trash can.

The presentation

On average, we present the client with three creative paths. To get those three, we generate, test, and discard many other ideas. When presenting each path, design stories are the starting point. We describe the concept, the process we followed, and the insights generated from our immersion in the subject. In the case of Rio Cello, each of the three paths were based on the idea of being "in between." Despite being more than three-hundred years old, the music genre of the event is between classical and contemporary. It belongs to all times. It's between traditional and

popular, between personal and universal, between simplicity and complexity—as an identity should be. It carries the simplicity of its essence yet is flexible enough to receive the complexity of a system.

We only present ideas we believe in. We'll never put forward a half-baked idea, or one we're unsure about, as many agencies do, so they end up inducing the client to choose their preferred direction. It's difficult for us to think of favorites when what matters most is whether they are relevant and respond well to the problem.

When we are blunt and consistent in what we propose, there's never a case where the client begins to micromanage our work. It's very simple: make a good design and present it with conviction. This builds confidence.

We've never been through a situation where the client doesn't like any of the creative paths because we always involve the client in our thought process before completing the presentation. The client gets to follow the entire process and often participates in cocreation workshops. Long before the presentation stage we've already returned to the client with a more detailed debriefing, with questions raised, and with possible solutions. This practice eliminates potential issues. Early in the Rio Cello process, we suggested sound and movement as a basis for what we'd produce, as that's what the project and its public identity were essentially about. We also shared a significant number of design stories with the client, so they were able to choose the ones that they thought made the most sense. As such, when it comes to presenting the three creative paths, the client's response is pertinent because they've joined us on the journey. There's no imposition of what we think we know about the client's business. It's something built together.

ID badges

Identity guidelines

As the world of commerce has changed, so, too, have guidelines. What was once rigid is now fluid, and flexible systems are essential, with intelligence and logic in their construction. They should be inviting and constructive, and open enough to transverse an unpredictable future. Gone is the time of a single, stamped form, and replicating it across each piece of marketing collateral.

On the other hand, it's important to clarify the thinking behind an identity because this gives direction to its usage. The examples in a style guide are usually good practices of combining the identity elements, and they also serve as inspiration—never to put creation in a cast, where it's immobile and still. We always contemplate a manual in brand and identity projects, even if it is reduced in size compared to what used to be the norm.

There's no way of ensuring that the work we create is what ends up on the street. We deliver a project, and it spreads out into the world, taking on a life of its own, like a child who has left home. The only exception is when every last part of a project is created by us, when we finalize the artwork, and when it goes straight to production under our watch, as with Rio Cello.

The first step to finding clients

Before everything else, build and launch a consistent portfolio based on where you want to be positioned in the market and on the type of work you want to do more of. You can showcase projects that involved low budgets, or no budget at all, but when you do the work, give it your best to achieve a quality of result that will impress. That's how you get those first doors opened.

Key points

A few things are vital to know: why your client is different from their competitors, what the client expects from the project, and what will determine a successful result.

When discussing the production of individual deliverables, always consider the effect your work will have on the environment.

As a lot of design can be open to interpretation, your terms and conditions can be hugely helpful when it comes to protecting your studio.

An invoicing option is to request 100 percent in advance for small budgets, 60 percent for medium, and 30 percent for large.

When negotiating with clients, imagine you have two baskets—one that holds what's open to negotiation, and one that holds what isn't.

Never change your work attitude based on the price of your proposal. Always give your absolute best.

Every project is an opportunity to show your curiosity and increase your knowledge.

Experiencing and experimenting make room for the unexpected.

To avoid pushing a client toward a particular creative path, only present ideas you believe in.

Letting your client follow the process with you can help to eliminate potential issues toward the end.

Guidelines should be inviting and constructive.

It's not always possible to ensure that what you create is what ends up on the street, so it can help to think of your work as a son or daughter who has left home and is making his or her own way in life.

RIO
CELLO

23°

AdAge

JUDANN POLLACK
DEPUTY EDITOR
T: 212-210-0458
M: 201-926-4691
JPOLLACK@ADAGE.COM
@JUDY_POLLACK

685 3RD AVENUE
NEW YORK, NY 10017
ADAGE.COM

OCD

New York
www.originalchampionsofdesign.com

Project: Ad Age

Launched as a trade publication in the 1930s, Ad Age has become a global media brand with headquarters in New York City.

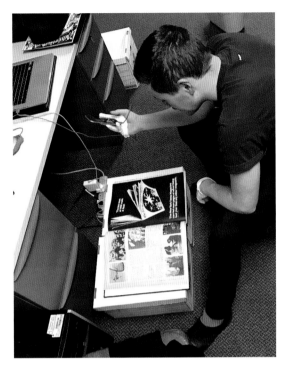

We spent a day at the Ad Age archives in Detroit, where they had issues dating back to 1930. White gloves were required.

When Josh Golden was hired as Ad Age's president and publisher in May 2016, Heidi Waldusky was brought on board as associate publisher and general manager. After the duo had been at the company for a year, they were ready to transition it from a publication to a brand. During their prep work, Ad Age's design director, Eric Spooner, brought Heidi an article in *Fast Company* about the work our cofounder, Jennifer Kinon, had done for Hillary Clinton's 2016 Presidential campaign. The article was heavy on process, detailing how she organized the team, and how they carried the workload with very few designers. Ad Age operates under similar constraints, with just two designers on staff. Heidi was interested in learning more about OCD and our branding work and reached out with a request for proposal (RFP).

When we respond to an RFP, we do background research on the organization to inform the scope. We don't do any design work until we've been selected for a project and fully engaged as an agency. Our contracts include an up-front engagement fee to ensure both parties are invested in the process.

The capabilities presentation
Following a successful RFP process, we then made our capabilities presentation, which fell on Valentine's Day. At least twenty people were in the room, including our founding partners, Jennifer Kinon and Bobby Martin, and our strategist, Sarah Hermalyn. To prepare, we researched how to map our process to their needs. We brought in a consultant, John Buysse, who had moved from the advertising industry into social strategy. He offered a great perspective on the industry and Ad Age's place within it.

Ad Age was interested in finding its digital voice, and wanting to work like a brand, not a trade publication. During our presentation, we talked about process and shared work we had done that demonstrated identity design's reach across print and digital.

Our proposals include research, strategy, design, and implementation. Those four steps are the same for everything we do.

Deliverables
Ten days after the pitch meeting, we were hired for the rebrand. Our proposals included research, strategy, design, and implementation. Those four steps are the same for every project we do; they're not revolutionary, but reliably efficient and effective. We charge flat fees for research, strategy, and design. Implementation fees are presented à la carte and decided at the end of the design phase during a planning session.

Our design exploration was reviewed in brand workshops
at the OCD office and with the client.

Ad Age was our broadest implementation project to date. We had worked on bigger design systems, but never with such a diverse collection of deliverables. Included in the project was the typical workshop, guidelines book, business system, and social media kit. Then it branched into the redesign of the magazine; the redesign of a series of publishing templates, including bound white papers and reports; a variety of newsletter templates for emails; updating the look of their website (more than one hundred frames); a membership and subscription tool kit for print and digital subscribers; tool kits for two events; a full video package; and Ad Age's annual competition trophy.

The whole project was completed in about eight months, from the first meeting until we went live. That's completely insane considering the scope of the deliverables. Most of our projects take two or three years, and this was one of many projects we were working on at the time. The phrase, "building the ship in flight," was used quite often.

The contract

When we begin our relationship with the client, we use broad strokes to outline the process, time line, and deliverables. When we reach an agreement, we capture the details in a formal legal document.

In any contract negotiation, each party has its own set of needs and values. For us, one particularly important detail is whether we're able to share the work when it's finished. The value of the project changes for us when it can be made public versus when it is kept confidential. There are so many ways to come to an agreement on value. Levers include fees, timings, and scope. Ultimately, you want have a signed contract that accurately reflects the relationship and expectations of all parties.

On pricing

Every pricing proposal is custom to the project. As a designer, you need to ask yourself what's important to you. Sometimes it's just to get the work and build your portfolio. When we started OCD, we didn't turn anything down. Whatever came in, we did our best to make it great and then get it out the door and into the world. If we followed any particular pricing model or special formula, we wouldn't have been able to create as many opportunities as we did.

The research phase

Ad Age launched in 1930, so it has an incredible collection of historical artifacts. Jennifer Kinon and lead designer Michael McCaughley spent a day at the Ad Age archives in Detroit where they studied issues dating back to the beginning. White gloves were required. Jennifer and Michael also spent a day at the office in New York where issues from the past fifteen years were stored digitally.

We went through absolutely every piece of print, marketing, and magazine ephemera that we could get our hands on to try to establish any patterns and find any typographic moments that we could draw from. We wanted to familiarize ourselves with the client so we could pull from their history rather than inventing a completely new style.

We conducted forty-one interviews to strip away any of our assumptions about the brand. We talked to staff to understand how everything worked within the publication, to readers to understand feelings outside the publication, to advertisers to understand why they were buying ad space, and to advocates to learn why they were so devoted and outspoken in their love for Ad Age.

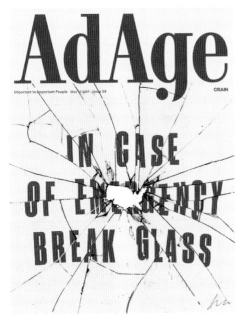

A small sample from the four proposed directions
we presented to the Ad Age team.

The strategy phase

For us, strategy is very much qualitative rather than quantitative—we don't put tons of surveys online, for example. Strategy is about finding logic in our observations from the research phase and streamlining them into an inventory of challenges and opportunities for discussion. Getting to know a brand is like getting to know a person: You can't discover everything over one dinner or by simply looking at someone. We ask questions, we spend time together, and we talk to fans and skeptics. We piece together a clear understanding of what the business or product or organization is and then we pick out the best parts and amplify them.

The design phase

Design is subjective. There's no single viable solution, no single best logo, but you know when you find one that works. We only present identity systems that we know will work.

We don't always present the same number of options. We want each idea to accomplish something different, to speak with a different voice, and to give the client a different outcome. That way, the client makes a business decision, rather than choosing a style.

Design takes as long as you have. You can always refine. You can always push further and further. Time plays an important role in every project, which goes back, again, to contract negotiation.

All our design work is derived from previous project phases. If the research and strategy is original and meaningful, then the design work will be, too. During exploration, we'll sometimes stray into areas where we think, "Oh that looks like something I

just saw." For the final art, we haven't run into any problems where we need to pull back on an idea because of potential copyright infringement because our research and, therefore the solution, is so specific.

Before we start designing, we'll consider common visual references with the client, as well as design styles, descriptors, tones, and intents so we have shared expectations.

The client makes a business decision rather than choosing a style.

On choosing a final direction

We take the hard line that we need to believe in every idea we present. So we're confident that whatever direction the client chooses, we're in full agreement that it's the right way forward. We then spend a great amount of time on refinement, development, and chiseling out something that everyone is extremely excited by. Occasionally we'll have a favorite option in a presentation and we won't shy away from identifying it. Everyone on our team comes up with great ideas, but it can be a shame when we present three ideas and two don't get made.

With Ad Age, we presented four very different

The redesigned identity was applied to the magazine
and a wide range of touchpoints.

directions: a refinement of the existing brand; a historic reinterpretation; a more avant-garde exploration; and a future-forward course, completely driven by where the client felt the brand was heading. We framed the four directions by presenting them in that way, telling the client that they all work stylistically. Then we asked, "Where is your business going? Which one best aligns with your intent for the work you're going to do in the next twenty years?" When choosing, clients should think about what their business needs are, not which system is "prettiest."

The Ad Age team papered an office with the design work so they could live with it for a while. They ultimately wanted to take some chances and be future-forward but weren't ready to give up their equity and visual history. We pushed two directions a little further before a decision was made and, after about forty-eight hours, an emphasis on curation won the day as it best aligned with the emerging editorial voice.

The "g" in the wordmark worked like a virtual paperclip. It offered a little metaphor, a little craft, a little equity, and a lot of flexibility. The system had to be a workhorse. Advertising moves fast. The news moves faster. With just two (now three), full-time designers on staff, Ad Age needed a rinse-and-repeat system that looked fresh every time. The bands of color were our solution: When they need a design element, they have all the stripes. When they need the design to get out of the way, they deploy fewer stripes. The bold colors can compete for eyeballs on the newsstand, in your office mail, or in your social feed.

The seventeen-color palette brought variability. For efficiency, we simplified the typographic tool kit. This is where we leaned on Ad Age's newspaper heritage. We kept it simple, with three typefaces and a commitment to easy-reading columns on all platforms. That's it. "Retina" for headlines, "Exchange" for body copy, and "Outsiders" for bylines and small details.

We've seen proof that the client made the best choice by their ability to execute the work. They know their business better than anyone. At the same time, our research and strategy phases help clients to better understand what design can do. We try to set the clients up for, "You've done all the hard work. You just need to pick one, and it's going to be great." Nine times out of ten they're prepared to do just that.

We asked, "Which idea best aligns with your intent for the work you're going to do in the next 20 years?"

On design execution

Rebranding Ad Age was very different from rebranding the Girl Scouts of the USA, which was very different

Event staging and digital layouts

from rebranding the Women's National Basketball Association (WNBA). They all have different forces at work to implement the graphic design. For the Girl Scouts, we knew the girls and their troop leaders would implement the designs. For the WNBA, we knew they had an army of vendors that were all trying to get on the same page. For Ad Age, we knew they only had two designers.

The way we build the system for each client takes into account the way the system will be executed. With our Ad Age design, for example, we created those horizontal strips and that color blocking so they had a plug-and-chug graphic system that just two people could use to release a weekly magazine. The volume of work they have is extraordinary. So, we discarded the crutch of stock imagery and replaced it with the branded element of energy and bright colors to fill that vacant space. We wouldn't have necessarily done that if we hadn't learned that they only had two designers who were struggling under the pressure. Branding can help to alleviate that pressure, and it can be a tool of efficiency that helps bring a team together. That can only be achieved by uncovering the right details during the research and strategy phases, so that we know when we're designing that the implementation will be efficient. We learned how critical that can be through our previous experience of working in-house.

Measuring the success of a project

We launched the Girls Scouts' rebrand with the launch of our company eight years ago, and we're still measuring how that system has flexed and grown, and how the fidelity has held up over time. What feels like success is when we're waiting in line

at the grocery store and we see a Nestlé bar with the Girl Scout branding on it in exactly the way we would've done it. Success is also seeing the mission of the business aligning with the purpose of the identity—seeing a client's business boosted by the redesign. That was something exciting with the WNBA, how the brand is now more embraced, and people are more familiar with WNBA players.

Each project has a different measure of success, and when we talk about branding, we talk about it being forever, so every year we go back and monitor things and occasionally offer to audit a brand or help the client to regain any lost efficiency. When we build a system, what we're really doing is using our research and strategy to make sure it's bulletproof when it goes to implementation.

Key points

There are four steps involved in all identity projects: research, strategy, design, and implementation.

From the beginning, make sure you have a signed contract that reflects the expectations of all parties.

Getting to know a brand is like getting to know a person. You can't discover everything over one dinner or by simply looking at someone. You need to ask questions, spend time together, and talk to the client's supporters and critics.

There's no single solution to anything.

Design takes as long as you have, so time is an important factor in negotiations.

Believe in every idea you present so that whichever direction the client chooses, you're in full agreement that it's the right way forward.

THE 'ANGRY BLK WOMAN' MAKES REAL WOMEN ANGRY

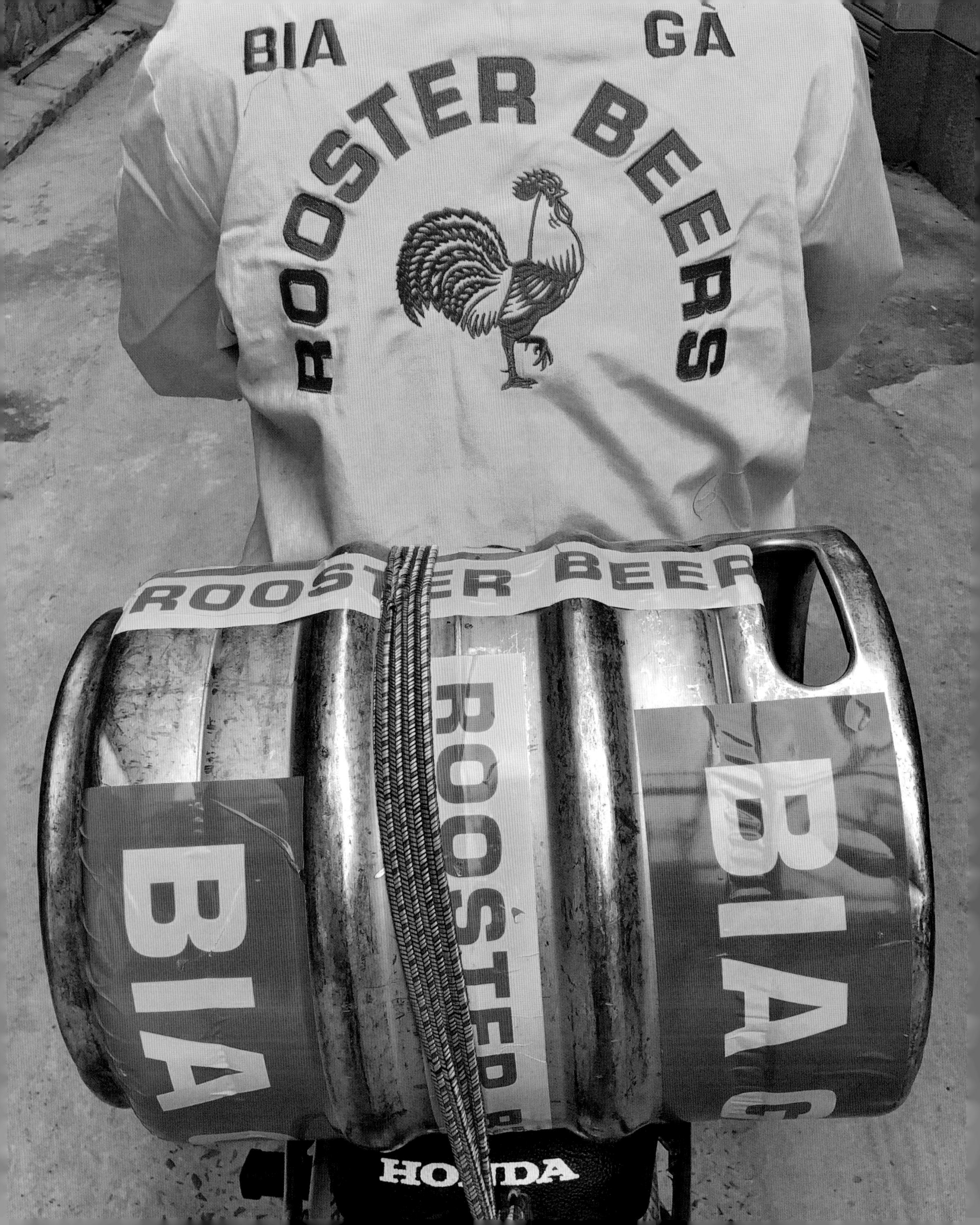
BIA GÀ
ROOSTER BEERS
ROOSTER BEER
ROOSTER
BIA
BIA
HONDA

Rice Creative

Ho Chi Minh City
www.rice-creative.com

Project: Rooster Beers

Rooster Beers was founded in 2015 on a small piece of land in Can Gio, Vietnam. It began with a 150 liter (40 gallon)-fermentation system that was built from scratch, and a tiny, cold room to ferment the beer. Eighteen months later, their capacity had grown to 2,000 liters (528 gallons). They don't use rice, sugar, cheap grain, or artificial flavors, and all their ingredients can be traced to origin.

PRIDEFULNESS   **HUMOUR**   **SUBSTANCE**

BEER

NET CONTENTS
12 FL. OZ. 355 ml

We zeroed in on three brand pillars: pridefulness, humor, and substance. These became boards of visual research that were added to by the whole team.

There's an established and buzzing craft beer scene in Vietnam, with many new brands cropping up. At the time, the scene was essentially foreign expats all making variations of beer, with exotic ingredients or strong flavors. Phat Rooster Ales, as our client was known before we worked together, had a strong association with the scene. We were approached by the founder, Michael Sakkers, and his new investor, Brook Taylor. Brook was adamant that we refresh the brand after seeing the value in our previous work.

Once we have a solid brief, we'll generate a scope of work that can evolve as we move through our process.

Our first task before receiving any payment is to write the brief with the client. During our initial client meetings, we ask a number of key questions, although, they vary as every project is different. Here we asked what the client was doing to make themselves stand out among the crowd and what

their relevance was to the local market. We needed to understand the viability and relevance of the product to gauge how we could become a strategic partner. Most clients come to us with a brief, but we challenge the details in it to ensure that, by the end of the meeting, we have the most appropriate brief to help solve the problem at hand. Once we have a solid brief, we'll generate a scope of work that can evolve as we move through our process. We propose different phases in the scope and often prepare a statement of intent to outline the opportunities we see before the project begins.

We offer an extensive list of services under the headers of brand development, visual identity system, applications, and communication. There are plenty of subheadings. The brand development and visual identity system usually falls under phase one of a project. When it's completed, we have a better idea of what applications will be needed in phase two, and then more phases develop as the working relationship continues.

Deliverables

We were hired to deliver research, brand strategy, design strategy, and the visual identity system, including identity guidelines. This predominantly included a website and packaging system, but the list of deliverables evolved as we worked with the client and grew our relationship. Many new ideas were proposed on how to launch the rebrand, and we created a slew of garments, uniforms, keg designs, and guidelines for social media.

We'll always have a general scope of design work before invoicing. It's subject to change while the process uncovers the design strategy. We make clients aware that potential changes might occur,

A glimpse of one research board

and, because we've previously explained our process, they're okay to adjust fees accordingly.

Terms and conditions

The laws in Vietnam are complex and usually favor the bigger companies. That's why it's essential that we have a solid contract structure to avoid needing to pursue legal action, as that road never leads to anything positive.

We don't negotiate our terms because they're always fair and, in our experience, they set the best possible tone for the strongest outcome. The project duration is based on the time we need to think deeply and conduct enough research, but not too much, because if a product drags, it's bad for efficiency. Sometimes clients imagine we like to take as much time as possible. That's not true. More often than not, project delays come from the client with their decision-making, or internal challenges. We stipulate the process because we are the experts in branding and design. We're sometimes asked to skip a step, but if we can't generate a scenario where we can do the best possible work for a client, we'd rather not do it at all. We don't like to waste anyone's time or energy, including our own, and we have graciously bowed out of many more projects then we have accepted.

We've developed a very straightforward paperwork policy, even when we work with friends. There are so many variables around a project that we like to keep paperwork, contracts, and agreements of any kind official. This doesn't mean we aren't flexible—we've worked in barter situations, for sweat equity, and accepted royalties as payment, for example. Although we'd love to shake on it and let that be enough, it's better for the health of our working relationships when we create a contract document, consult a lawyer, and have our clients sign on the line.

Individual contracts often need revisiting because a branding assignment is essentially a process of discovery. As an example, an established architectural practice hired us to create a new visual identity for them. We began with our in-depth research, and we were well on our way to creating a design strategy. Our clients, a duo, hadn't really taken the time to step back and consider their practice in more than a decade. The research we conducted opened their eyes to what they had become and, for whatever reason, persuaded them to put their practice on hold while they made a return to formal education for another master's degree. So instead of designing their identity, we ended up creating templates for books that would house their thesis projects. Needless to say, we had to make a new contract.

When clients query the terms

This is something that often happens. It's easy to assume that our clients will understand our work. In the vast majority of cases, they do not. We have to carefully explain why it takes time to research. We have to explain that to make a website, we might have to hire a writer or photographer. "Third party costs may apply" always raises eyebrows. We have to explain that if we engage a photographer, we also need to charge an art director fee. There are so many factors in our process that can surprise someone who thinks they simply need graphic design.

Many clients are unsure about all of it. We respect, and must never forget, that our clients need to have a little blind faith in us. It adds to the sense of responsibility we feel when engaged in a project,

One of our sketch boards

especially as our fee is sometimes a massive amount of the client's funds, and the brands we work with can be our clients' lifework.

On pricing

Basically, we have an overhead and we need to turn a profit. We know the amount of work involved in a project and we divide our operations into hours. We also understand that what we hand over at the end of a project could end up being almost priceless for the client. Try to separate your favorite brands from their visual identities. How would you evaluate that property in dollars? Consider that we're not just talking about a logo and a tone of voice. We're talking about the strategy that led to the identity—the thing that makes it all work. We get involved and help to shape our clients' businesses, which is extremely valuable, so we keep that in mind when setting our fees. I don't think we've had a client who ever felt overcharged after four to twelve months of working together, even if they started out by saying, "Wow, that's expensive." An investor in a large brand we recently helped to shape took us aside and suggested that next time we charge much more.

We begin by charging a fixed fee, at least for a chunk of the work. It shows client commitment and it's good for cash-flow, but more often than not, we end up in some sort of retainer situation with our clients where we continue with new scopes of work. Think about the right time to say goodbye to your clients. Although you might think it's after the delivery of brand guidelines, that's when so much creative work is about to begin.

Our cost structures also depend on the finances of the client. Some clients have planned ahead by allocating certain amounts for fixed payments, whereas others don't know how much of an investment they need to make. We're quite flexible, though, we'll work out the best method for both parties.

Try to separate your favorite brands from their visual identities. How would you evaluate that property in dollars?

When to increase rates

Our rates increase every year. A few factors contribute to that, such as inflation, increased overhead costs, and so on. We started out with pricing that was low because we were doing something new in our market and we had trouble justifying proper fees. At the time it was okay, because we were just two partners, and we had no qualms about suffering to build a business. As soon as we had credibility from our finished work, we could raise the rates and begin to educate the market. When we began hiring staff, there was no question the fees would increase. Paying people to have a good life and a nice environment to work in is a priority. Now we have budgets for items such as company trips, dinners out (for twenty people),

Various sticker designs

and books for the library. There is no questioning the importance of these things. It's the culture of a company that's built on its people. Keep them happy.

On client negotiation

Negotiation is usually based on payment terms, not the actual project fee. A reduction in budget for the same number of deliverables would result in us needing to bring in additional work to fill the gap. Consequently, the project in question would suffer from a lack of attention.

Estimating the time frame

At the beginning of any project we give our clients a general time frame, e.g., research, three to four weeks, strategy, two to three weeks, and so on. It almost never takes the exact time. We aim to get work done as quickly as possible, without rushing, but clients themselves typically extend the deadlines.

The Rooster project was completed fairly quickly. The first phases of research, strategy, and visual identity were finished in about two months. We have, however, been working with them ever since, rolling out new ideas and smaller tasks, consulting on strategy, and running their social media accounts.

Invoicing and payment

For every payment, we issue an invoice (designed using Adobe InDesign). We rarely send a receipt as the invoice acts as a receipt for most of our clients.

Our scope of work and payment schedule are all broken into milestones. For example, the completion of research and strategy is one milestone. We are paid a percentage of the overall cost to begin and finish that. We then move into identity work and are paid another percentage upon completion.

We accept most methods of payment and generally charge in U.S. dollars, even for our Vietnamese clients. The fee gets converted into Vietnamese dong once we draft a contract. That's required under Vietnamese law. In some cases, we can charge in other currencies if it suits the client better. We don't really mind absorbing the exchange rate.

The research phase

Rooster Beers was an up-and-coming craft beer maker, in a market experiencing a craft beer boom. We began by looking into the competition, but quickly exhausted that task, determining that these other businesses were in a bit of a dogfight. Our investigation could then focus around our client's story, daily routine, vision, and inspiration. We researched the history of beer, both globally and locally. We looked at beer drinking habits in Vietnam, where the brand would always be rooted. We looked at the way other good, simple products have communicated universally.

We quickly uncovered that Rooster Beers (their new name) was sitting on a fantastic opportunity but was hindered by an identity that was off the mark. Rooster was the only beer maker in the market that was focused on making great, classic beers for the Vietnamese consumer. The competition's products were centered on exotic ingredients. In a nutshell, Rooster was making a range of everyday beers that could compete with the mass brands, while the competition was making niche, artisanal beer that had more appeal to an expat consumer.

Even before doing much of a deep audit, it was clear that Rooster's image at the time was catering to the same audience as their competition. The brand was communicating with what we deemed as the

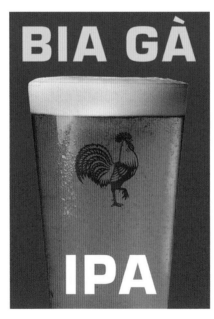

The range of Rooster Beers

"American Craft Beer Convention." We suggested erasing almost everything, and focusing the communication around a simple, fresh range of beers for a local market.

The strategy phase

We often begin by conducting interviews or giving clients a questionnaire to fill out. Although we've gone through these sessions many times, the questions are never stock. Every case is different, and the questionnaire takes quite a lot of time and effort for it to be effective. Once this opens up topics for debate, other types of research begin working in tandem. We uncover a strategic opportunity that can focus the creative work. The opportunity might, very simply, be the concept that drives each design decision. This is what keeps the work strategic.

Rooster Beers became about being a working man's beer. Design for design's sake would be much too distracting. We just wanted the brand to look like beer. We researched and categorized the conventions of beer design, making sure we amalgamated nearly all of them into our design before stripping it all back. Somewhere behind our thoughts of research and strategy, we actually wanted designers to dislike the outcome. We felt that if we could avoid the comment, "great design," we would have created something effective for the client. The result is a bit anti-design.

Generating ideas

In the studio, we have an enormous wall of pinboards. Projects get quite tactile, and we make sure that the team never feels like there's a limit on space for visual exploration. For Rooster, we zeroed in on three brand pillars: pridefulness, humor, and substance. These became boards of visual research that were added to

by the whole team. That part of the process involves a lot of free association, and it builds up an extensive bank of material that gets sifted and funneled into various design decisions. This is the unquantifiable part of the project where process and art-making converge.

If we ever feel like we're in a creative rut, we'll revisit the verbal branding documents we've created. We might also pull in fresh minds from elsewhere in the studio.

The concept that drives each design decision is what keeps the work strategic.

When to stop experimenting

The foundation of the Rooster visual identity system meant it was almost creating ideas on its own, but visually, we couldn't strip it back any more than we already had. At this point, we were done. There was some sense as well that polishing it too much would be unhelpful. There's an inherent carelessness in the outcome that's actually rather good. We had great Vietnamese copywriting that we wanted to prioritize and the foundation of a visual identity system to use it. The work was lively, making both us and the client laugh.

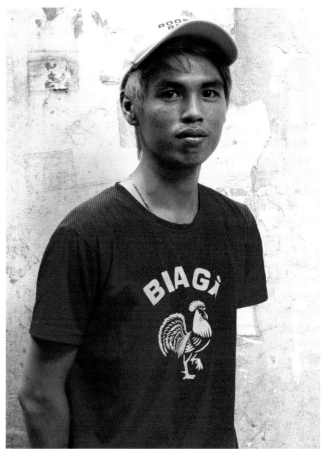

The list of design deliverables evolved as our relationship with the client grew.

Presenting an idea

Our presentations are crafted using Illustrator, Photoshop, and InDesign, and we'll often use various mock-up tools, such as LiveSurface, for showing the work in context. We do our best to avoid wasting studio hours, so if a design idea can be accurately described to a client in words, it will be. If it needs a visual reference, we'll prepare that, too. Sometimes we feel strongly that an idea is the right one for the brief, and our designer expands it into a full design system for presentation.

As the client approves each step in our process, and as the preceding steps tend to lead us to a single design suggestion, we often only present one idea. It depends on which stage of the process we're at, and what we're presenting. For instance, if we're creating a brand name, we'll propose several options that have all come from our naming process. If we're presenting a visual identity system, there'll be one main driving idea, but there might be options with the typography or the color.

The design direction is often already spelled out when we present our ideas for the verbal branding, positioning, and strategy, so while we have backup ideas in place, we always share the main idea that we think best solves the problem. There have been times in the past when the client hasn't accepted our idea, leading to a few never-ending stories where the work was reduced to the whim of the client's unsound feedback. We learned the hard way how to create the process we now have to keep the work strategic and on track.

Our experience has given us more confidence to push back against comments that can potentially disrupt a strong solution, but we don't have the attitude of always being right. We form an equal partnership with our clients about creative decisions. That said, we sometimes have to remind our partners that the work isn't actually for them, it's for their audience. We completely sympathize with the client feeling incredibly personal about their brand, but, to an extent, it's important that they let go. Clients we advise in this way always end up thanking us.

On copyright and trademarking

It's up to our clients whether they want to collaborate with a trademark attorney, as that's not our line of work. With law, there are guidelines, and then there are opinions. We help our clients to avoid risk, but we're also conscious of too much legal advice harming the work. In an open case in the studio, a trademark attorney advised us against moving forward with our client's first choice from a naming process because the name was deemed too common. We advised the client to have faith and plow forward, as the greater identity would do its job to properly differentiate the brand.

In another case, we crafted an incredibly simple trademark for a client to visualize their brand's core concept. Someone in our studio discovered that the mark was extremely close to a number of unrelated, but well-known, trademarks. So, we put our work in a line-up with the other accidental, but perceivable, infringements. In the end, the client was so committed to the mark that they decided to move forward with it.

Developing guidelines

The work we complete will often result in the provision of style guides, whether for the verbal

Multiple stickers give a distinctive look to Rooster kegs.

brand, the visual identity, or for social media activity. All our guides allow flexibility because things evolve over time, and it's far more helpful for a client if you anticipate this change in advance. It's good practice to think ahead, to leave aspects of the branding open for new adaptations. We remind our clients to check with us when they're unsure about implementation, even if it's many months after completion. We're finding that clients are increasingly asking us to have a brand guardianship phase for a few months post-launch, when we review the work done by in-house teams, or we act as the in-house team until one is formed. Sometimes the relationship just never ends, and we continue as the brand's design team.

We remind our clients to check with us when they're unsure about implementation.

On studio marketing

Most of our first clients have come through word-of-mouth recommendations, so as you're starting your business, invest time and effort in making your early projects as thoughtful as possible. A happy client will bring you many more clients.

Key points

From the outset, it's important to understand the viability and relevance of your client's product to gauge how you can become a strategic partner.

The brand development and visual identity system can fall under phase one of a project. When that phase is completed, you'll have a better idea of what applications will be needed in phase two, and then more phases can develop as your working relationship with the client continues.

It's possible that the initial scope of work will change when the process uncovers the design strategy.

Having a solid contract structure in place is essential for avoiding potential legal action—nothing positive ever comes from that.

Your working terms should always be fair, setting the best possible tone for the strongest outcome, so don't feel that the client can make you change them.

Contracts may need to be revisited throughout a project because a branding assignment is essentially a process of discovery.

When a design idea can be accurately described to a client in words, do it. You can get a much quicker feel for whether it's a strong direction to follow.

As the client approves each step in the process, you can find that the preceding steps tend to lead to a single design suggestion, so it can be normal that only one idea is presented.

An equal partnership should be formed with clients regarding creative decisions, although as designers we sometimes have to remind the client that the work isn't actually for them, it's for their audience.

It's good practice to think ahead and leave some aspects of the branding open for new things.

GIẢI
CỨU
GÀ
TRỐNG

BIA GÀ

MAKE
BEER
GREAT
AGAIN

ROOSTER BEERS

CH
N
BIA

BI

THERE'S
ALWAYS
ROOM FOR
A COCK
OR TWO

ROOSTER BEERS

BIA
GÀ
ÒÓO
!!!

BIA GÀ

BIA

ROOSTE

LO
ACCI

BIA GÀ,
BIA
CỦA MỌI
NHÀ

BIA GÀ

COCK
-A-
DOODLE
DOO

ROOSTER BEERS

G
C
C
TR

ẬT Ử U GÀ

À

GÀ

BEERS

LY
MED

IU
U

NG

PROUD LOCAL

ROOSTER BEERS

BIA GÀ ÒÓO !!!

BIA GÀ

BIA GÀ, BIA CỦA MỌI NHÀ

BIA GÀ

MAKE BEER GREAT AGAIN

ROOSTER BEERS

THERE'S ALWAYS ROOM FOR A COCK OR TWO

ROOSTER BEERS

CHẤT NHƯ BIA GÀ

BIA GÀ

Foreign Policy

Singapore
www.foreignpolicy.design

Project: Gallery & Co.

Gallery & Co. is the official museum store at the National Gallery Singapore, with a bookstore, restaurant, bar, and design store in a continuous space. It fuses art and design into a curated retail experience offering books, design collectibles and prints, homeware, fashion, and children's products, accompanied by the Gallery's exclusive line of merchandise to complete the museum experience.

The project involved interior and space design,
as well as merchandise design.

We were approached by the client following a recommendation from another client. It's typical for us to get our business this way, so referrals are vital. It's why our key to success is to make sure we put every effort into all our projects.

Initial questions

When a client gets in touch, we always ask them for their vision of where their brand will be in the next, say, five or ten years. We also want to know how they think design will help them to give us a better understanding of their design knowledge and so we can explain things in the most appropriate way.

Our initial questions are generally the same for all of our identity projects, despite some jobs being smaller and more straightforward than others. In the beginning, we always try to establish what the client wants to achieve with their brand, as well as the specific deliverables they want us to prepare.

Terms and conditions

We don't normally start work until we receive a scanned or physical signature on our terms and conditions contract and the down payment is in our bank account. The initial payment is a demonstration of good faith from the client—we know they're fully engaged with us.

Although our working terms help set ground rules at the outset, there was a project we had five or six years ago where the client simply stopped communicating. As they were in another country, it was difficult to pursue, and we suspect it was a case of them running out of funds. These situations happen in every design firm at some point or another. There have been one or two incidents during our eleven years in business where we had

the option of using legal means to pursue payment, but we decided against it.

Every client is different, and sometimes they'll query our terms. It can be something as simple as whether payment is due in fifteen or thirty days or the number of studio copies the client is supposed to supply to us at their cost. Now and again, the payment schedule will need a little negotiation, too. It's nothing out of the ordinary, as our contracts are quite standard.

We always ask clients for their vision of where their brand will be in the next five or ten years.

Knowing what to charge

Pricing is usually based on how much we charged previously and a rough estimate of how much work and time is involved. One good reference point is to have a sense of what it takes for you to run and operate a sustainable business, including labor, overhead costs, cost of goods sold, and profit. When you've worked for at least a year, knowing how many projects you've accepted annually provides a good starting point to ascertain a rough range of how

Progress shots from the interior fit-out

much revenue each project should yield. Multiply the number of projects you expect in the upcoming year by your estimated fee to give the desired annual income. Remember to factor in the profit you want to make, otherwise you could end the year with nothing in the bank. Time is always crucial, too, and if you expect the client to be a difficult one, add a "headache fee." Inflation and the cost of living will also affect sustainability, and although nobody has asked us to justify rising fees, we did have one client who said, "You guys are getting more and more expensive every year."

We normally charge a flat fee based on our skills and experience. As the structure of design companies widely varies, only you will know what fee is too low, and what's too high. Money isn't the only thing you can earn. We once worked with a new gym that needed help with basic branding, and we traded our skills for gym sessions.

Most clients will want to negotiate, just as we negotiate with our suppliers. It's normal. We're all running a business. If we sense that our counterparts aren't negotiating in good faith, however, we walk away.

Estimating the project duration

The time a project is expected to take will be largely informed through experience of past projects. For example, it will become clear that concept development will take three weeks, not three months or three days. Eventually, every designer will reach an equilibrium depending on how they work. Once that's developed, it becomes rather easy to estimate the length of a project, but it's never perfect. For Gallery & Co., we worked backward on a time line based on when the project needed to launch. From there we

devised a strategy to fit what needed to be done into the available time line. All in, the project took about four and a half months from start to finish.

Handling payment

Whether we invoice in full or divide the amount depends on the project. It's pretty standard in the industry to separate the cost into 50 percent at the beginning and 50 percent at the end. Sometimes we work with other percentages that can be paid across the project duration. We use QuickBooks software to help facilitate the process, and 99 percent of the time we accept payment by bank transfer or check. There's never been an instance where we refused a client's payment method.

We don't vary our payment process for clients in other countries but, depending on the client, we do invoice in foreign/local currencies. Sometimes overseas clients can only pay in their local currency. We're generally not too concerned with fluctuations in exchange rates as we consider it one of the costs of doing business.

Conducting research

We don't prescreen our clients before we start a project. Sometimes we just walk into the meeting and start the conversation. Other times, the most we'll do is to take a two-minute look at their website.

When we start the project, the type of research will depend purely on the specifics of the task. Two things we definitely do are to look at the market conditions and audit the competition and comparable offerings.

Giving yourself the best chance of fulfilling design briefs needs an honest matching of problems with skills. If the client wants a well-performing website, then the project needs skills in user experience

Signage and wayfinding

(UX) and user interface (UI) design, a knowledge of technology, an understanding of the products on sale, and so on. To arrive at the most successful outcome, you need to be honest with yourself about having the appropriate skillset. This is crucial. If there is a good match, then the project will likely be successful. If there isn't, it's much better to walk away than to risk your reputation.

The design brief

The brief is put in place after we receive the initial payment because it needs work on our side to ensure it's effective, and we don't work until the client gives that show of monetary faith. Strangely enough, the number of times when clients provide their own brief is low. Perhaps 40 percent of the time they'll come to us with a brief in hand. Often, they only have a vague idea of what they want to achieve from working together. There are no headings or categories that are set in stone—they differ from project to project, client to client, and problem to problem. Take the example of a website—two clients say they want one, but what they truly want can be as different as day and night. So, every brief must be bespoke.

Ensuring a strategic approach to design

"Strategy" as a word has been thrown around in myriad ways and all sorts of circumstances and is, unfortunately, highly abused. Cutting through all the jargon, strategy is essentially about having a plan. When the plan is clear, the chances of success will be high, because we all know what we need to do and we won't be distracted. There's no magic potion here. The trick is to simply seek to understand the client's brand and vision. It's only ever possible for us to work on a client's brand when we understand its ins and outs, and when we're clear about what the client wants to do with it (if they already have an idea).

Cutting through all the jargon, strategy is essentially about having a plan.

A merging of strategy with visuals is generally an attempt to rationalize the design decisions. Say it's a gym. We'll first determine its personality and then the choice of typeface, color, and art direction will go toward supporting that. There are days when that's a real challenge. A bank, for example, may want to communicate integrity, trust, and that they're "here for you" and "in it for the long haul." That's difficult, and we try not to over-rationalize our choices in line with particular brand traits if our explanations begin to feel like a stretch.

Generating ideas

Sometimes five to eight of us will gather at our studio purely to brainstorm on one project. It's key to provide a safe environment for everybody to speak up as sometimes there's a tendency for someone to belittle or shoot down another person's idea. Never let this happen. It will quickly smother the generation of ideas.

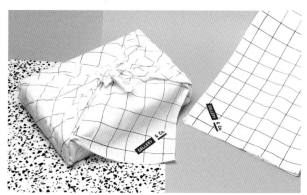

Key graphic elements that form the visual language include
basic shapes and rudiments, such as the circle, line, square, and
triangle, with a bright palette of blue, green, yellow, and red.

If we ever find ourselves unable to think of different approaches, we walk away. We do something else. We don't think about the project for a while. Sometimes the break can be as quick as an afternoon, and other times, it can take a few days. Walking away works like magic when the mind is allowed to wander. You'll be surprised how solutions can so easily pop into your mind when they're not forced.

We stop experimenting when we're happy with what we have and when the client's happy with what's presented. We've been fortunate in consistently achieving that.

Copyright and trademarking

We have never purposely checked to see whether there's anything out there that's similar to our work. We're not sure whether a scan makes any sense as there are trillions of designs in existence. It's practically impossible to create something that bears no resemblance to another design. Although the Tokyo 2020 Olympic logo, which was changed following plagiarism accusations, is a classic example of how copyright enforcement can go wrong. We've never collaborated with any trademark attorneys. We simply hand our files to the client, and if registration is a direction they want to take, they handle things from there.

The presentation

We have a standard process in which we'll present the client with our creative direction. It explains our vision and why we think it makes sense. The presentation is usually formed in InDesign, Illustrator, and Photoshop, combining words, images, and designs—anything that allows us to communicate our idea.

We show the client two ideas. Sometimes three, but usually two. Never five or ten. We find that two generally works best for us. We tell the client in our advance talks that they'll see our vision, rather than a set number of ideas. The key is to ensure that one of the two or three options hits the mark. It's not about quantity, but about that one killer bullet.

It's practically impossible to create something that bears no resemblance to another design.

Reaching consensus

Only present what you are comfortable with. We don't recommend putting out anything that you won't stand behind. So, if it's three ideas, they must all be your babies. We don't throw our babies out. Only show what you are truly convinced has met the design brief. That way, there's no need to steer your client toward a particular idea.

We're quite open in our dialogue. Some clients will make more comments than others. Some will make odd comments on colors and typefaces—usually the less sophisticated clients. We will talk them through it. Some just want to say something. They feel that it is their contribution. Let them have it, so they can feel more of a sense of ownership over the outcome.

The brand concept is based on the idea that the gallery is an "entrepôt of visual dialogues," harking back to early Singapore's role as a trading port.

It's extremely rare for us to have a client who isn't happy with any of the directions we present—something that again goes back to the key nature of referrals in our business. If push comes to shove, always, always, always ensure that any parting of ways is amicable.

Identity guidelines

Your guidelines need to be fairly prescriptive because a brand cannot be ambiguous or subjected to different interpretations. Decide well in advance which items are cast in stone and which have a degree of flexibility. Be clear about it in the guidelines. Whether we provide clients with a style guide depends on the budget. They're always prepared in PDF format, and we always recommend having one, because after we hand the steering wheel to clients, a guide will help them to avoid driving wildly without direction.

Communication with your client is key for ensuring that the work we do is the work that's implemented upon completion. If the work we have produced needs some adjustment to satisfy the client after the project is finished, at no additional cost, then so be it. We do it. Ultimately, we have to accept full responsibility for our work. Nobody else will.

Working with the right type of client

Although this sounds difficult to do, it's important to seek out clients who allow you to do your work as a designer. When you work with people who don't appreciate or value design, the process becomes a very difficult battle to win, and you'll be constantly cajoling your client into making the best design decisions based on your experience. If you get a good client at the beginning of your time in business, make sure you do the best job possible. From there, build a portfolio of consistently good work. View your first few projects as portfolio pieces to help you attract and get good, long-term projects. When your work is good and makes an impression, referrals will follow. The magic with a referral is that the business is almost in the bag because the new lead comes knowing that you've already been vetted.

Key points

Ask your clients for their vision of where their brands will be five years from now.

Also ask how clients think design will help them, as their answers will give you an understanding of their design knowledge.

Don't start work until receiving a down payment.

Money isn't the only thing you can earn. Skills can be traded for mutual benefit.

Don't be put off by clients who want to negotiate your fee. It's normal.

While it can vary, standard practice in the design profession is to split invoices into 50 percent at the beginning and 50 percent at the end.

The type of research that's conducted can depend on the specifics of the task, but be sure to look at market conditions, as well as audit the competition and comparable brands.

Brand strategy is essentially about having a plan.

If you find yourself unable to think of different design approaches, walk away and do something else.

Only present ideas that you're comfortable with.

Co.

←

ART
BOOKS
CULTURE
DESIGN
FOOD

Exhibitions
Programs
Study & Research
Collections

Art
Museu

Underline Studio

Toronto
www.underlinestudio.com

Project: Art Museum

Art Museum at the University of Toronto is a new institution that brings the Justina M. Barnicke Gallery and the University of Toronto Art Centre together as one entity. It's one of the largest gallery spaces in Toronto for visual art exhibitions and programming.

Art Museum location, with banners
showing the previous identity

Underline has worked with many organizations in the Toronto art community, so there were people at Art Museum who were aware of our studio. This situation is typical for us, as most of our work comes through word of mouth.

Initial questions

At the interview stage, before we prepare a proposal, we ask the client a lot of questions about what they would like us to deliver, what they're looking for in terms of design direction, who's involved in the decision-making process, and what's currently working (or not). For Art Museum, much of the discussion focused on how they were situated within the university. Their position was complicated in that there were two galleries, both associated with different colleges and significant benefactors, and all within the framework of a large university, its politics, and its brand. How they were going to create their own unique identity within all this complexity was a big question.

Deliverables

Art Museum hired us to design the brand identity, including guidelines, signage, a brochure template, stationery package, the website design and development, a digital newsletter, marketing brochure, invitation, and advertising templates. Signage was a critical part of the project. Although the two galleries were just steps away from each other, visitors found them difficult to find and to move from one to the other. Despite the galleries existing in busy, populated areas of the campus, there was little awareness of their collections. As such, color and boldness became a tool for creating awareness and helping the brand to stand out among the historical campus buildings. Budget was a concern, but we managed to work in the existing signage framework and, through color and contrast, we created eye-catching solutions.

Before payment

We always start a project based on an established schedule, even if we don't have a deposit. We never deliver anything or release files until payment has been received. If there are delays, our studio manager follows up. Having a colleague deal with clients on billing allows our designers to focus on design.

Having a colleague deal with clients on billing allows our designers to focus on design.

Terms and conditions

Our working terms are contained in a single-page document that has sections for fees, cancellation procedure, copyright ownership, changes and approvals, confidential information, as well as samples and promotional ability. We ask our clients to accept our terms with a physical signature on the proposal, although in many cases we accept email confirmation.

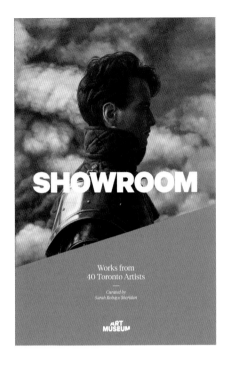

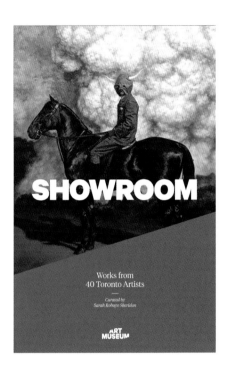

One of our early, rejected design ideas,
and a glimpse of our process board

Our payment schedule is a 35 percent deposit to begin work, 35 percent at delivery, and 30 percent within thirty days of delivery. Payments are generally received by check and direct deposit. In most cases, we quote in Canadian dollars, but for American clients, we'll quote in U.S. dollars and absorb the exchange rate fluctuations.

We have long-term clients who might not pay in the exact terms outlined, but we often reach the stage at which we know it's just a matter of time before we receive payment. This method was much more stressful in the early years of our studio when cash flow wasn't as strong as it is today.

Knowing what to charge

We begin by approximating our hours and trying to account for all the tasks of the project: research, design, meetings, press approvals, changes, and so on. We have consistent time frames that we always use as starting points (for example, three to four weeks for initial conceptual development) that are then adapted to any specific project deadlines or needs.

The complexity of the project and the deliverables involved are an important consideration with pricing, too. Proposals are often broken down into the cost per deliverable, and we outline the steps taken to arrive at the finished identity or application. If appropriate, and as a way to reduce our involvement or fees, we may suggest providing a template in Word or InDesign to let the client carry out the ongoing development of a particular deliverable.

When it comes to a potential negotiation, we wouldn't want to lose a good client because we were inflexible. However, we also can't take a loss. In most cases, we can revise the deliverables, or the process, to try and work to a client's budget.

Research, strategy, and experimentation

Building on the two galleries' distinguished histories, the Art Museum organizes and presents a year-round program of on- and off-site exhibitions, as well as intensive curricular engagement and educational events.

We have consistent time frames that we always use as starting points (for example, 3-4 weeks for initial conceptual development).

The museum sought a new brand identity that would emphasize its placement in the city and its engagement with both the university community and the greater Toronto public. We created an identity program that's built upon an angled logo and functions across a range of promotional collateral, including brochures, programs, posters, banners, and a website. The logo is set at the same 16.7-degree angle as the street grid of Toronto, firmly situating the museum in its location.

Our initial palette preference (top), the 16.7 degree angle of the
Toronto street grid, and the final palette after the client insisted
on avoiding yellow

Art Museum had gone through a strategic process prior to working with us that included input from key stakeholders, surveys of visitors, and an assessment of its relationship with the university and associated colleges. We reviewed all of this information and asked questions of our own to formulate a creative brief for the work. We use a set of strategic questions for the briefing stage, and we tailor the questions per project and client. When a client hasn't gone through an in-depth strategic process (with interviews, SWOT analyses, and so on) and it's clear that one is necessary, we'll collaborate with an external strategy partner.

The design phase

As we explore concepts and review designs, we always have a board of competitors' logos beside us. We also keep a list of keywords nearby that are pulled from the earlier strategy work, helping to ensure that we meet our clients' strategic needs.

Knowing when to stop experimenting generally comes down to time and experience. We sometimes show our work to people who aren't as close to the project to get their input.

When we presented the selected concept to Art Museum, we felt strongly that the color was perfect. We'd chosen a vibrant yellow that we thought would be very visible on campus and highly adaptable in various color spaces and usages. The client disagreed, saying it wasn't right, and there was a lot of back and forth. We presented a second round that used the yellow along with a broader palette of colors. Again, the client rejected it, insisting we drop the yellow. We were extremely disappointed because we felt that our preference was the right way to go. Moving forward, we then created the palette that we have now

and, in hindsight, we're so happy the client pushed back. The brand colors are playful, bold, versatile, and do exactly what they need to do for the identity. The palette is a big part of the identity's success.

It's important to show how the identity will perform in a variety of contexts.

Presenting ideas

We submit very polished concepts. For Art Museum, we presented the logo with its application to signage, brochures, and stationery. Showing how the identity will perform in a variety of contexts allows the client to better imagine how the work will look after implementation.

The number of options we share with the client depends on the project. If we're working on a magazine redesign, for example, we generally show two directions, which might differ in display typography and grid layout. For editorial work, we never offer more than two options because the complexity of elements coming together takes a huge amount of design time. For identity projects, we always present at least three ideas.

We always present the concepts in the context of the original strategy. This means starting the

Museum signage

presentation with a recap of the brand personality, the audience, and the goals of the rebrand. We recently instituted a studio rule where we don't tell clients which idea we prefer so as not to influence them one way or another. We really want their feedback and to gauge their reactions. What we do, however, is talk through the pros and cons of each direction and what we think each idea communicates.

Referring the client back to the brief is always our first method in taking away the subjective element. That doesn't always prevent micromanagement, but we've found that discussing feedback in person makes it easier to explain why we did the things that we did, as well as understand any underlying concerns.

Referring the client back to the brief is always our first method in taking away the subjective element.

When the client doesn't like the work

In some cases, we've presented our directions for an identity and then had to create a second presentation of additional concepts. We don't normally charge for the second round, but we ask for more direction than we might have received in the first round because we want to know why things didn't work, and in what direction we should take new ideas.

The Art Museum process was complicated. We began with a brief and then after the first presentation of concepts, it became clear that we couldn't satisfy our client's desire for simplicity with the brand elements they said were necessary. At that point, they were working with the name "Art Museum at the University of Toronto," so we were required to include two institutional logos as well as the full names for each gallery. The project was paused, and the client internally assessed what was necessary for inclusion. They came back to us with a revised list of requirements and a commitment to "Art Museum" as the single brand name.

This rethink helped us enormously for our second look at the brand. We no longer felt constrained, and it seemed to us as if the identity could now achieve what the client wanted—a strong, simple, and bold brand. Because of such a change in the design brief, and the redundancy of our early work, we needed to charge additional fees.

Our original schedule for completion of the project was six months, from briefing to website launch. After many delays, extensive internal approvals, a rethink on the name, and the massive job of pulling together the website, the new branding launched ten months after our briefing, and the website took almost two years to go live.

On guidelines

We supply a prescriptive set of guidelines in all of our completed brand identity projects. Most of the time it's a simple, eight-to-ten page PDF that outlines the

We're so happy the client pushed us to revise the palette,
as the colors are a big part of the identity's success.

visual elements of the brand as well as their usage. The cost for this is included in our fee for the overall identity. For larger brand projects that require more substantial guidelines, we price the document separately and supply a more extensive PDF (perhaps thirty to forty pages).

How the branding will be implemented and carried forward can influence our creative decisions.

How the branding will be implemented and carried forward can influence our creative decisions so it's vital to know these details very early in the process. For our designs to succeed, they need to be realistic for the company that's using them. We try to be as detailed as we can in the guidelines, and we always offer to review PDFs of any follow-up work our clients create in-house.

How to find new clients

The best way we get work is by word of mouth, which is ideal because there's already a certain level of built-in trust. If clients don't believe their projects require a high level of design, the process doesn't go well. We're committed to producing work at a certain level that's demanding of the content and production. If the client doesn't have that same commitment, then we're not a good pairing. Any marketing we do is more about creating awareness of our existing work—photographing it well and submitting it to blogs, award shows, and books. We've never had much success when targeting specific people or companies.

Key points

Don't release any final files to the client until payment has been received.

If you work as part of a team, having a colleague deal solely with clients on billing lets designers focus solely on design.

A potential payment schedule is to receive a 35 percent deposit to begin work, 35 percent at delivery, and 30 percent within 30 days of delivery.

When negotiating with a client, revise the deliverables or the process you work through to try to fit with a client's budget.

You don't always need to present your client with a set number of identity options. It can depend on the project.

After you present more than one design direction, if you first keep your thoughts to yourself on a potential preference, you can hear feedback without influencing client thoughts.

For a design to be successful, the effort required in its application and rollout must be realistic for the company that's using it.

Floor nature

32 class / AC4
1380 × 191 × 8 mm

25
РОКІВ ГАРАНТІЇ
YEARS WARRANTY

Diamond

32 class / AC4
1380 × 191 × 8 mm

25
РОКІВ ГАРАНТІЇ
YEARS WARRANTY

Premium

33 class / AC5
1380 × 191 × 8 mm

Fedoriv

Kiev
www.fedoriv.com

Project: Rezult

Korosten MDF Plant in Ukraine is an environmentally friendly factory producing laminate flooring and medium-density fiberboard (MDF) panels. Equipped with cutting-edge Siempelkamp machinery, the plant operates large storage facilities, a traffic network, and its own utility systems. It stands among the top-ranked Ukrainian companies that used to export its products to Russia, benefiting from its favorable location near a major southeastern railway hub (Korosten, in the Zhytomyr region).

Photos from an early visit to the production facility

Korosten MDF Plant contacted us in 2006 when they opened their production facility. They wanted their branding to communicate that they were a local, wood-friendly business. We created an extremely simple identity—the logo comprised three green trees in a lockup with their brand name. According to the client, it was exactly what they needed. Job done.

A decade later, due to geopolitical change in the relationship between Ukraine and Russia, the Russian market was now closed to our client. It had been one of their main sales channels, so they wanted to discuss a rebrand.

Since our initial 2006 meeting, the client had improved the quality of their product, and they were now ready to embrace a more international focus. They weren't certain which target markets would be open to them because of the geopolitical climate, but they wanted to project more of a European outlook, with the potential of selling worldwide.

For all our projects, early involvement is crucial. With Korosten, there were a couple of meetings to understand the brief, and a small team of ours spent a day at the production facility, approximately 124 miles (200 km) from our office, to discover how the wood is processed and the product is created.

Initial discussions
It was immediately clear to us how deeply involved the client wanted to be in the project. The curator was the main shareholder's daughter, and the shareholder was personally involved, too.

As an aside, critical to the success of our agency is what we call the "father approach," meaning that we try to focus our efforts on owner-run businesses and insist on having direct access to the main shareholder. We employ the approach

in approximately 80 percent of our projects. In developing markets in this part of the world, people are still very hands-on, even when they have businesses with revenues of more than €100 million ($116,000,000). They're the founders, and because they're fully engaged, they like to be involved in the branding. With branding and positioning projects, discussions should always be at the CEO level.

With branding and positioning projects, discussions should always be at the CEO level.

Sometimes, however, the people at the top don't want to be involved. They say, "Okay, I need to sell more. I don't care what you do. Get the work done." In those instances, we liaise with people in middle positions, such as a marketing manager or director. Despite having zero shares, they'll behave like they own the company, meaning they are process-oriented, not result-oriented, so they're prepared to take risks. They're creative leaders with the "father" attitude—ready and capable to lead the process of creating something new, and with the power to make decisions. In a traditional corporate structure, there

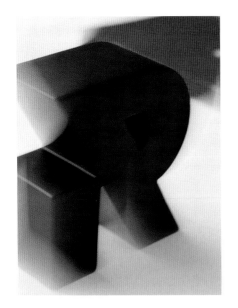

Various identity elements following our rebrand

are too many people with the authority to say no, but not yes. This is the wrong type of partner for us. If the middle person has the authority to approve the project, then we're happy to deal with them.

In our discussions with clients, we asked how they feel about themselves and their product. We pay particular attention to the balance of rational and emotional responses. There are rational benefits to any project outcome, such as becoming 10 or 20 percent more price effective, but we look for something more. From an identity viewpoint, if a client focuses on the rational benefits, the designer tends to think the project will be dull and unattractive, preferring to work on something that incites more passion.

If you focus on the rational aspects of a project and elevate them so high that they elicit an emotional reaction, however, you begin to appreciate them. For example, you visit a technical museum in Germany and see machinery built at the beginning of the nineteenth century and you really understand that this came from an era when designers were actually industrial engineers, not, for example, interface designers. That's exactly what we experienced during our visit to our client's facility. The production process was so huge that it was difficult to imagine the machines. The industrial facility was more like a spaceship than a normal factory.

Pricing our work

We undertake creative consultancy in two main areas. The first, our main competence, is working on brand-based change projects. As examples, we collaborate with the biggest Ukrainian government-owned retail bank, with 6.3 million customers, and we work with the leading Ukrainian postal company, which is privately owned. They approached us because their consumers and the market conditions were changing faster than they were.

Clients might say, "We need to rethink ourselves, our main idea, our differentiation point, our human resources, and our culture to better satisfy our customers." In our view, marketing today is not the science of how to push products from producer to consumer, but rather the art of predicting what the consumer will want tomorrow, and changing the organization, products, and experiences you offer to meet those future needs.

The first phase in a change project is critical, when we take a "deep dive" into the client's business to understand their brand, market, consumer, environment, positioning, and vision. You can't skip it. Many clients want to proceed quickly, but we'll respond, "Okay, if you want us to create things now, give us the brief and we'll move onto tactics. We'll create the campaign for you. If you really want to create change, give us an opportunity to fully understand what's going on. If you don't want to spend so much time, money, and effort on analysis, research, interviews, and so forth, what do you expect will change? If you want quick results, let's do tactics, but we don't call it change. Change will come in three years, after months of understanding what you want to change."

These change processes start from €150,000 ($175,000) and increase according to individual requirements. It's here that we involve ourselves in a client's entire digital ecosystem, understanding how they integrate customer relationship management into their website, who works with the data, and how they use the data. This is a deep, long-term project, lasting three to five years on average.

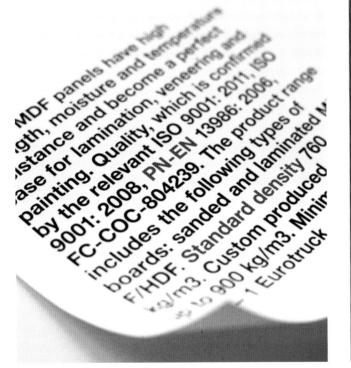

Identity elements and ephemera

The second area we deliver is branding. For us, that means the client has their own product or service, but what they sell needs to be packaged. (Rezult is a good example.) For branding, we work on positioning, identity design, and communication. The client wants us to help craft their visual, tangible world. This kind of project starts at approximately €50,000 ($58,000), depending on specifics. The average time frame is three to nine months.

Don't touch a project unless you believe you can do great things.

Client negotiation

We almost never negotiate the fee in the branding process because it's crucial to produce the work in the right way. What we can negotiate is the number of elements we develop. For example, when you have a hotel, there might be one hundred and twenty elements to its brand design. A new restaurant might need fifty elements, whether it's a leaflet, menu, signage, website, iconography, uniforms, and so on. On the other hand, a niche business may only need ten or fifteen critical elements.

You can need money, you can want to sell more, but you should never sell anything that doesn't match your methodology, even if the client insists, because it

can negatively influence the final result. For us, that's one of the secrets to building a strong agency.

Our understanding of how professional work begins is simple—you either believe, or guarantee, that you will do the work perfectly, or you find risks and refuse the work. Don't touch a project unless you believe you can do great things, even if you need the money. If you do accept it, then don't call yourself professional.

We've taken on projects after ignoring the red flags and they became laborious. That's why we pay close attention to the chemistry in meetings and discussions, especially for our change projects. We average four to five meetings with a client before we make a deal. It's rare when we meet the client and they say, "Okay, how much?" "This." "Okay, let's shake hands." Rare, but not unknown.

Our founder, Andriy Fedoriv, once struck a deal twenty-one minutes after meeting the client for the first time. They met in a restaurant, each knowing a little about the other beforehand. The client owned a huge food production company. They started to talk and the client said, "According to the moon calendar, today is a very good day to start working together. Let's do the following: Today I will give you a down payment of €10,000 [$12,000]. I insist. And then we will decide what we want to do together." It was Andriy's fastest sale.

We're not afraid of losing potential clients. We don't like when it happens, but we understand that choosing the clients we like and the projects we believe in is the only way to build a business. Our goal then is to foster a long-term relationship.

Our main source of pride isn't the international awards we've won, but that we have clients who have worked with us for many years. We have a client

Packaging

whom our founder began working with one year before he launched our company, and the working relationship has continued for nine years without a break. Every month we've done something together. It's a big challenge to nurture this kind of relationship and to keep the client passionate about it because when you're a little tired, the easy option is to think fresh blood can add something new.

Research

With Rezult, it wasn't necessary to carry out research into consumer behavior. Instead, we worked closely with our client's sales department. We interviewed managers from their retail partners to understand what they wanted, and we let them judge our prototypes. The process needs a trusting client who can give us enough time for concept development. When clients start a project, they want to see results as soon as possible, but we always give ourselves enough time to work on our visual concepts.

The design idea

For Korosten, we wanted to create an identity that people would associate with the German-speaking part of the world—efficient, disciplined, and well-organized. Why? Because that's the kind of attitude we saw during our visits.

Changing our mental nationality— our preconceived beliefs and attitudes about a nation— is a very productive creative tool. This is done by thinking about the feelings, attitudes, and perceptions the customer will have when they see the product. For example, private labels can sometimes be misleading. Some may pretend to be Swiss, so they incorporate the red and white cross of the country's flag and use the word "Swiss."

Deceiving people isn't the way to elicit a desired response—you can achieve this through design. We imagined that our creative office was situated in the German cities of Stuttgart or Dusseldorf, and we imagined ourselves as someone our client should be seen as—a German engineer—not the shareholder we dealt with or his daughter because as well as owning the production plant, they are also deeply involved in successful fashion and hotel businesses. We asked ourselves what kind of identity we would expect and determined that it wasn't about being human or modern, but about being incredibly sharp in our production process and how we treat and display our product.

Changing our mental nationality is a very productive creative tool.

One of the things we spoke about with the client was the action of cutting because when you work with wood, that's the main part of the process. It's mostly the slicing process that delivers the ultimate quality. When we proposed the use of a cutting theme in the project, the client was fully on board.

We came up with the name Rezult. We wanted to insert an error, using z instead of s, giving a knife-like

Caps, jackets, and the team strip

property to the lettering, as if it's lifted directly from the cutting process. The z became the main graphic element of the type. We didn't want to create a separate, alternative symbol because that would add an unnecessary element.

When our projects involve brand naming, we present five to seven names.

This concept resulted in a red, white, and black palette, with sharp positioning based on cutting and the tagline "Stand on Quality," with each of its meanings: to persist in being a quality-driven company; quality as a passion, not just a characteristic; and the image of physically standing on quality, as you physically stand on the product, the wood flooring.

The client presentation

We almost always present in person. Last year, we worked on a branding project for a client in Saudi Arabia, and it was the first time we were successful when we didn't meet the client in person. It can be common to work remotely when you do smaller tasks, but as we focus on branding projects with a huge amount of implementation, involving a major change in the life of a corporation, the face-to-face dialogue is vital.

There were two main presentations for Rezult—the naming and the design. Although we always present names separately from the creative work, we try to speak about the mood and emotional territory of each option and illustrate them with various references. That's why when the client accepted Rezult as a name, and our lawyers said it was available to register, it was already clear that we had moved to a more rational design direction with a focus on engineering.

When our projects involve brand naming, we present five to seven names before narrowing them down to one, two, or three. In the naming process, the main problem isn't the creative aspect, but the registration because the chance that your name is available to be registered is very low. We advise our clients not to fall in love with just one option. Ideally, after presenting, we send two or three names to our lawyers because it takes time and money to check and prepare the documents, and this time eats into the design schedule. If we want the project to move forward without unpredictable stops, we want to have a plan A, B, and C. Sometimes we've already registered two out of the three names we've presented to the client so that no one else will use them. The client can then negotiate ownership with us. With Rezult, we only registered the one name and, thankfully, it was available.

For the design presentation, the client normally will know in advance how many different ideas they're going to see. Our approach is to deliver two options, left and right, rather than try to impress clients with

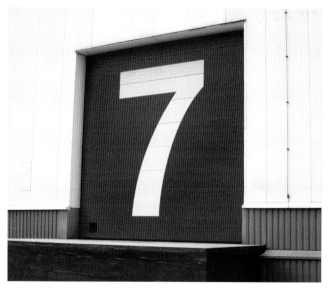

Wayfinding and building graphics

six or seven ideas. Some agencies will bring eight very similar options to the table. To fully develop the concepts we believe in, however, it's important to focus on one or two directions. When it's two, we make them radically different. Rezult is a good example, with "human" and "natural" on the left, and "robotic" and "engineered" on the right. That mind-set of having different outcomes influences the design. You can't merge the two because if you try, the result can end up being very average.

For the design presentation, our approach is to deliver two options, left and right.

Measuring the outcome

Our client strongly believes that since the launch of the Rezult name and identity, one important figure in their annual turnover has changed—the export market increased by 30 percent.

After the rebrand, the Rezult team also felt that communication with their clients became much smoother and more constructive. The marketing

support they could offer dealers, including point-of-sale displays and catalogues, became an important sales tool when reaching agreements and signing contracts.

Key points

The first phase in a "change" project is crucial, involving an in-depth look at the client's business to understand their brand, market, consumer, environment, positioning, and vision.

Any negotiation in the fee for a branding project is based on a change to the number of elements that are developed.

Choose the clients you like and the projects you believe in because it's the only way to build the portfolio you desire.

When trying to achieve consensus in traditional corporate structures, there are too many people with the authority to say no, but not many that can say yes.

Where brand naming is concerned, it helps to have a plan A, B, and C, while advising clients not to pin their hopes on one name in case it can't be registered for copyright.

When delivering two design options, make them radically different. If you merge the two ideas, you'll end up with something very average.

Clients are normally in a hurry, but it's important not to rush any project.

Marketing today doesn't revolve around how to push products from producer to consumer. It's the art of predicting what the consumer will want tomorrow.

STAND
ON
QUALITY

Fraher Architects

#21
Floor 3

Up stairs / First right
Hello—

020 8291 6947
mail@fraher.co
Fraher.co

Freytag Anderson

Glasgow + Oban
www.freytaganderson.com

Project: Fraher Architects

Fraher is an award-winning architectural practice in London, with the ability to analyze, conceptualize, design, produce, and deliver spaces and architecture in a fully integrated package.

The Etch House, by Fraher

Joe Fraher of Fraher Architects was a client of our cofounder, Greig Anderson, when Greig worked under the moniker Effektive. When Freytag Anderson was formed, Joe came to us for an identity update. Most of our clients find us through word of mouth, whereas many actively look for the design they want in places that have surprised us (on Behance and Pinterest, for example).

When potential clients get in touch about a project, we generally send them a briefing sheet to glean the information we need to start work. It's essentially a questionnaire that saves us time and acts as a stimulus, challenging clients to seriously think about what they want, because sometimes they're not actually sure.

The briefing sheet acts as a stimulus, challenging clients to really think about what they want.

Part of our job is to articulate the client brief, so we supplement our questionnaire with a face-to-face discussion to understand the motivation behind a design commission. When we get to know the people we'll be working with, we always learn more about their industry. That's one of the best parts of being a designer.

The Fraher project began with a briefing sheet and lots of discussion.

The proposal

After we determine that we're a good mutual fit with a client, we invest time preparing a detailed proposal. It's a document that sets out the context and parameters of the project in a digestible way, giving clarity to costs and time frames. Each proposal is followed by a design agreement that commits the client to the project and then an instructing invoice that kicks things off.

Our project proposals are informed by the design brief. We normally summarize the brief and incorporate it into the proposal along with a breakdown of deliverables and an outline for our possible approach to the work. The Fraher deliverables included the brand identity system, stationery suite, website, and internal templates. We occasionally undertake revisions of the proposal to fit changing budgets or specific items to deliver, and we always issue a final proposal, design agreement, and instructing invoice before starting work.

The time frame

Every project we do is given the same level of importance, regardless of budget. If we accept a piece of work, we take the time to get it right. Sometimes there's a natural solution waiting to be discovered, sometimes it takes longer. With Fraher, we told the client it would take three weeks, but it ended up being closer to five with the website build incorporated.

Website

Setting terms and conditions

When we first launched our studio, we cobbled together terms and conditions (T&C) from our experience of studio norms. When we could afford to hire a lawyer, we had our own drawn up. T&C have their place—they can protect your intellectual property (IP)—but more important, they tell a valued client your ideas and processes and that you are willing to uphold them. We ask clients to agree to our terms with a physical signature. We're old school that way.

Fairly often, we have clients query our terms before work begins. Queries are generally about wording, because they've inevitably become harder to understand after being drawn up by a lawyer. Normally a brief conversation is all that's necessary for things to proceed. Requests for amendments are rare.

A few times in the past, projects haven't quite gone to plan. The most notable was when a client wanted to cancel the project midway through and pursue an altogether different direction. Our T&C helped us to bill the client for the work that was already done and also protected the IP of the designs we created. The client chose to pay for the IP and then closed the project, which was an acceptable outcome for both parties.

It's only happened once when we've needed to pursue legal help to get paid. This was because a client ceased all correspondence after we handed them the design files. We had no other choice than to pursue them in court. Luckily a couple of strongly worded letters from our lawyer did the trick early in the process.

Design agreements and contracts can only protect you when you're willing to spend the time and money to pursue them. Thankfully, the majority of people commissioning design are decent and respectful.

Pricing

We have a studio day rate, but we generally work on a project fee basis. The reality of designing means that sometimes you're reliant on factors out of your control. This approach covers us for the less productive days.

To reach the right fee, we take a number of factors into account—particularly the length and complexity of a job. If we take on a project, it's because we want to do it, and we've been known to agree to staggered payments with startups and the like.

Our studio fee normally includes two concept designs, and also optional items that may not have been requested in the initial brief—items we feel can help support the overall outcome. These could be recommendations toward achieving the project goals or specific design deliverables.

Every project is treated individually, and although we're always open to negotiation, there's a fine balance to tread regarding common sense. A project that provides an opportunity to reach a new market, for example, can be more important than a higher-paying one. Pricing is always difficult. We've only changed our day rate once in five years, and that was informed by client feedback and the experiences of other designers.

Handling payment

We always ask for at least a third of the cost up front. When we complete the concept design we typically charge an intermediate 40 percent, leaving 30 percent for a balance payment. We prepare invoices using FreshBooks, and although we use email to acknowledge receipt of payments, we don't send formal receipts—that's something we've never been asked for. Bank transfer is the norm for our clients

Brick House, a single family dwelling in North London, lies within a prominent Conservation Area. The client wanted to open up the dark cellular lower ground floor spaces towards the garden. Maximizing natural lighting at lower level was of key importance in the design proposals, whilst sinking the tv snug into the darker spaces within the plan.

Categories
Residential

Architect
Fraher Architects Ltd

Joinery

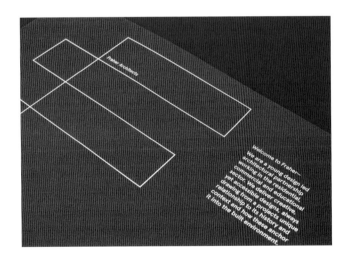

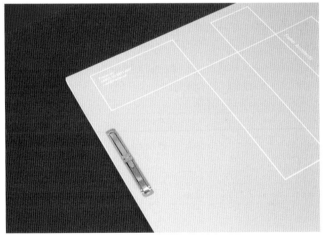

Website and stationery

sending us money, although we wouldn't say no to cash. Beer has also been offered.

On research and strategy

The Fraher project was unusual because we already knew the client from a previous job. Normally our design strategy is informed by various sources, the most relevant and reliable of which tend to be verbal—ordinary discussion or, for more complex projects, client workshops.

Sitting down with the client to discuss the project provides them with an opportunity to contribute directly to the design process. This applies throughout the project, not just at the beginning. We strongly believe the best and most successful projects are those that the client feels they have mutual ownership of.

The best and most successful projects are those where the client feels they have mutual ownership.

Our discussions are supplemented with desktop research, looking for insights that aren't obvious—the things the client is perhaps too close to notice. These insights tend to have that elusive ring of authenticity that's so useful when creating or developing a brand.

Design isn't rocket science, although it sometimes wants to be. We find the best strategy is to get to know the client, what they do, how they do it and, perhaps most important, why. What audience are they currently talking to? Who do they want that to be in the future? When those questions are answered, the rest follows pretty quickly.

When it comes to merging strategy with design, interpreting brand values, traits, and positioning in a visual sense is an instinctive part of every designer's job. The written voice for a brand comes naturally, in the same way. For us, these aren't items that can be extrapolated into a formula.

Generating ideas

It helps to let ideas simmer. Read the brief, meet the client, and then do nothing for a few days. This lets you think about a potential solution indirectly, from the inside. Then when you're ready to start designing, you've got a few ideas to chase around a sketch pad.

When to stop experimenting

Our cofounder, Daniel Freytag, was once told by his first creative director that the greatest skill a designer can have is to know when to stop designing. Knowing when comes down to confidence and experience. Sometimes you just know when the work's complete. Equally, you know when it's not.

Copyright and trademarking

In our design agreement we state that we take all reasonable steps to ensure that our designs do not infringe upon others. In reality, you never know.

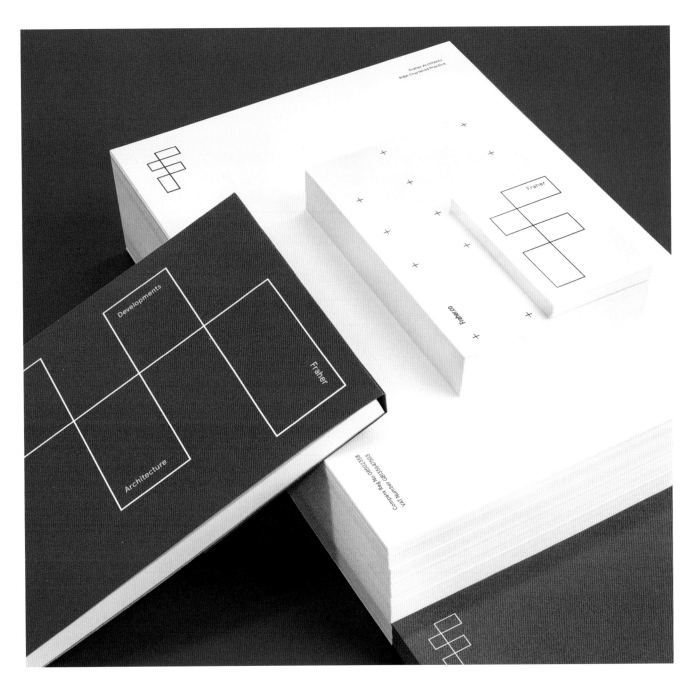

Stationery

This is a hot topic that will no doubt get hotter because we live in a world where everyone sees everything. The visibility of (good) design has vastly increased. A spread in awareness of what constitutes quality work can only be a positive thing, but this new visibility also invites problems.

It's surprising how often two designers on opposite sides of the world, with a similar project in hand, can come up with a similar design by sheer coincidence. Twenty years ago, no one would be any the wiser. This is no longer the case.

This situation raises interesting questions. Are like-minded designers unconsciously drawing on a common pool of influences? What's truly original? How many configurations of line and color can studios realistically consider?

All you can do is stay true to your own design values and be flexible enough to change direction in a pinch. Fortunately, there have only been a handful of projects in the past where we had to change direction because of potential infringement.

Regarding the trademarking process, we went through it during a side project for the HeyWow! children's books. The process was relatively straightforward—we submitted our design and waited for the necessary checks to be done. It took two months, costing approximately £200 ($260).

The presentation

Whenever possible, we present our ideas in person, using a polished PDF presentation. We use various tools, such as Yellow Images, for turning our ideas into digital mock-ups. Don't get carried away, though. If the idea isn't going anywhere, it's a bad use of time.

We rarely show more than two concepts and sometimes just one. The number is set out in our proposal along with the amount of amendment rounds included in the fee.

It's important to fully develop an idea, test it, and make sure it's both evocative and practical. Being focused from the outset helps us streamline the whole process and avoid subjective conversations about design. Of course, if a client is unhappy with a concept, we'll go right back to the beginning.

If you can rationalize your ideas, and provide sound business reasons for design choices, clients will listen.

The rule is to never present something that you're not entirely happy with, though there are always cases when you prefer one concept to the other. If we have a preference, we try not to let it influence our presentation, but perhaps inevitably, the client can sometimes tell. Quite often, they'll ask us to name our favored route.

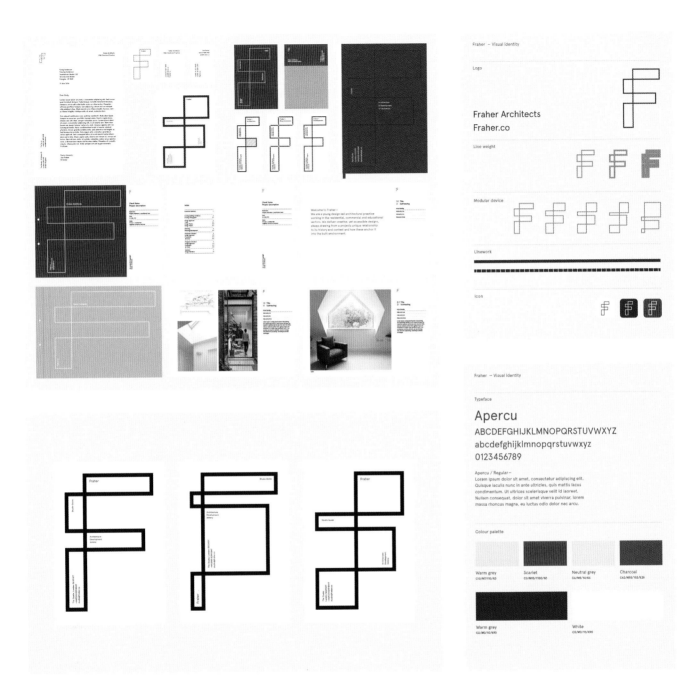

Logo

Fraher Architects
Fraher.co

Line weight

Modular device

Linework

Icon

Typeface

Apercu

ABCDEFGHIJKLMNOPQRSTUVWXYZ
abcdefghijklmnopqrstuvwxyz
0123456789

Apercu / Regular –
Lorem ipsum dolor sit amet, consectetur adipiscing elit.
Quisque iaculis nunc in ante utricies, quis mattis lacus
condimentum. Ut utricies scelerisque velit id laoreet.
Nullam consequat, dolor sit amet viverra pulvinar, lorem
massa rhoncus magna, eu luctus odio dolor nec arcu.

Colour palette

Warm grey	Scarlet	Neutral grey	Charcoal
C0/M7/Y10/K0	C0/M95/Y100/K0	C0/M5/Y4/K6	C62/M55/Y52/K28

Warm grey	White
C0/M0/Y0/K90	C0/M0/Y0/K0

Guidelines

Client feedback is important and should be noted. We've all had the conversation about what color they like, but ultimately, if you can rationalize your ideas and provide sound business reasons for design choices, clients will listen. Don't be afraid to say no, but tell them why. Keeping design routes to one or two also helps limit the inevitable red herrings.

Thoughts on guidelines

If the client is happy with a design, they tend to be very protective of what we've created for them and are keen to enshrine the work in a guideline document. This won't encourage experimentation, unless experimentation is part of the system.

We offer guidelines in PDF form as an optional extra, but some projects are too small to warrant a formal guideline document.

To heighten the likelihood of your work being implemented exactly as planned, you need to gain the client's trust through the project. Be a nice person to work with. Explain approaches clearly, in layperson terms, so that they're easy for clients to understand and defend. If you've done those things, the client will continue to look to you as the custodians of the design.

On measuring success

We've recently started asking questions that relate to business performance and impact, and we're trying to add a debrief document to each project to capture this important information. It'll help us with our new business activities, demonstrating the success of our work in a tangible way.

Finding your first clients

Try to get your designs seen by as broad an audience as possible using as many channels as possible.

Instagram, Twitter, Behance, and Pinterest are all great visual platforms, but they're not conducive to letting you express your design thinking in words. This is much more difficult, so it's no surprise that most designers are bad at it.

We use a mix of LinkedIn, Medium, press releases, and blogs to share our thinking. They let us communicate to potential clients a little more about us, our approach, and what we might be like to work with.

Key points

Initial client questionnaires can save time and can challenge clients to think about what they want before hiring you.

A proposal document sets out the context and parameters of the project in a way that's easy for the client to digest. It should give clarity to costs and time frames.

Even if you have a studio day rate in place, identity work is generally carried out on a project fee basis that includes a set number of concepts (two in this case).

The payment schedule requires that at least a third of the total project payment is needed up front.

The most successful projects are those where the client feels a sense of mutual ownership.

The best strategy is to get to know a client, what they do, how they do it, and most importantly, why.

As a designer, sometimes you just know when the work's complete and ready to present. Equally, you know when it's not. Draw on your experience.

Fraher

Fraher Architects
RIBA Chartered Practice

Fra
RIBA Charte

itects
ctice

Bedow

Stockholm
www.bedow.se

Project: Fable Skateboards

Fable Skateboards is a skate brand launched in 2017 by Daniel Björklund. He wanted to create a new type of company within the skateboard culture, one that takes responsibility. Half of the company's profits go toward charitable purposes.

Pattern and logo sketches from the development phase

Daniel, who runs Fable Skateboards, is a former client of ours, and we've collaborated a lot over the years. It's typically likc that: people move from one job to another and they come back to us. Or our clients recommend us to others. Sometimes we'll get emails from potential clients who have seen our website or Instagram feed.

The initial meeting

Before sending a quote, we usually meet the people we're going to work with during the design process. This is preferably in person, but sometimes through a video conference when dealing with an international client. We explain our philosophy, how we work, and we show some previous projects that we think are relevant to the client's business. At this stage, we mostly want to get a better idea of their product or service, and to know how their business model looks.

Knowing what to charge

Pricing always depends on a variety of circumstances. Fable Skateboards is a startup and was a low-budget project, but there were benefits for us that didn't involve the money: It was for a good cause, with half of the company's profits going to charity, and the client was open to pushing the boundaries of how a skate brand could look. This gave us a project that has won several design awards. Ultimately, low-budget work is okay if there are other values involved, but we never accept unpaid projects because that means the client isn't properly invested in the design process, and it can sometimes lead to your hard work being flushed down the drain.

After running a studio for thirteen years, we know what to charge in accordance with industry standards. Generally, we increase our rates every two years.

Clients will sometimes try to negotiate our fee, but it's not very appreciated. We're a small studio with reasonable prices, and we never want to overcharge. At the same time, we understand that clients have limited budgets, so we try to be open to different pricing ideas. As mentioned, money is one currency, public relations could be another, and creative freedom yet another.

We never accept unpaid projects, because that means the client isn't properly invested in the design process.

Charging by time or by project?

The simplest way to set your rates is to charge by the hour because people understand the idea of time costing money, and the more hours spent on a project the more expensive it will be. In reality, this is far from ideal. The process behind coming up with a name or design idea can sometimes be two hours, while at other times it can be eight weeks, but it's worth the same amount to the client regardless of how many hours you spend. It's normally better to look at what the project is worth to the client and to their brand.

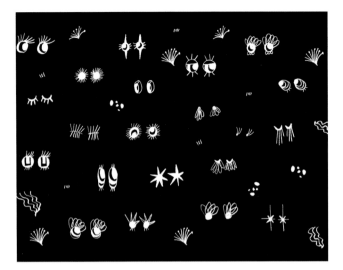

Illustration and typography, brought together for the website

Additionally, as you gain experience in the design profession, you learn what paths to take during the design process. As that shortens the time involved, it results in a personal disadvantage when you charge by the hour. Bad design takes a lot of time because inexperienced designers are indecisive.

Invoicing and payment
Our quotes and invoices are created using InDesign. We usually charge 50 percent of the total fee at the start of each project, with 50 percent due upon delivery. The down payment gives us the time and security to do our work without feeling stressed about the financial aspect. If the project stretches over a long period, we split the second fee into two 25 percent payments.

We once worked with an artist who only had a budget for printing and no money to pay for the book design. We traded our skills for an art piece instead, but it's not recommended. When clients pay with money, they show that they value your work.

Regarding payment and process, there's usually no problem working with clients abroad. Digital tools have made it easy to communicate and fairly easy to present the work. Getting paid by our American clients is problematic, as there always seems to be an issue receiving wire payments from the United States.

Terms and conditions
Having clients agree to our working terms via email is normally enough for us, but with our larger projects a physical signature is preferred. A visual identity is quite an abstract thing to invest in. It's not like buying a car. So you need to specify in detail what's included in the scope of work, and it's essential to clarify expectations from the outset.

Estimating the project time frame
For the work to be great, it needs to run through certain phases. We start with strategy, where we determine what and how to communicate. Then we come up with a concept and a visual idea before beginning the actual sketching and designing. When a strong, relevant design idea is developed and fine-tuned, we develop a system for implementation. Time frames usually depend on two things: the budget and the deadline. The bigger the budget and the longer the deadline, the more research we can conduct and the greater the variety of solutions we can produce. This only works to a certain extent. Limitations are often a good thing because if the deadline is too far away, it can be difficult to maintain focus.

For the Fable project, we didn't have a deadline, and the budget wasn't massive, so there was pressure to complete the work without dedicating a huge amount of time to it. We took the client through each of the different stages in our process, and the project lasted around three months from when we got the assignment to the end result.

Conducting research and setting the brief
Our design process always starts with a client workshop. When, in collaboration with the client, we find out what and how to communicate, the answer is boiled down to a keyword that, alongside one or more selected emotions, helps build the concept that the design will be based upon. We also look at the client's competitors because it's always good to move in the opposite direction. We analyze what they're saying through their identities and, in Fable's case, most competitors appeared very macho, using skulls, flames, and so on—clearly communicating to a male

Custom skateboard designs with brand illustrations

audience. We wanted our design to steer clear of such stereotypes and be much more inclusive and non-gender specific.

Following the workshop, we provide our clients with a PDF summary, which is refined into a design brief at the end of the document.

The headings in the brief can vary, but we usually want to address these five questions: What are we going to do? Who are we speaking to? What is our core message? What feeling(s) do we want to communicate? What should the overall result be? When we know the answers, we can start creating a concept and a visual idea.

Translating strategy into design

We use the concept we uncover in our strategic phase to answer all the different design questions we bump into throughout the process.

The idea for Fable was to distance our client from traditional skate culture, instead focusing on being friendly and inclusive. This complements Fable's business model, which is to donate half of its profits to the purpose of creating an inclusive and open skate community.

The hand-drawn, illustrative style, warm colors, and typography have a naive and unpretentious feeling, chosen as a deliberate contrast to traditional "tough guy" skate graphics.

The brand name comes from the word "fables"— the short stories in which animal characters teach various moral lessons. Fable has its own set of friendly-looking characters that appear throughout the identity.

When to stop experimenting

Our designers are given a brief with a key narrative.

Then it's up to them to translate that brief into something visual. When the designer has something to present, we look at it together and, if it is understandable and visually appealing, we can move forward. "Understandable" and "visually appealing" may sound vague, but that's where experience comes in—the creative director can usually see quite quickly what is suitable to present to the client.

Similarities to pre-existing designs

Our process tends to result in a unique outcome. That said, we see the same things as everyone else, and it's hard to not be affected by your surroundings. In the past, we've unintentionally created something with similarities to other designs, but we'd never release a project if it is too close to what we've seen in existence. We've always taken pride in creating our own work, and we constantly try to do things differently from other design studios.

The presentation

Because we involve our clients as much as necessary through the process, those who hire us almost always trust our knowledge of design. As long as we stick to the given strategy, there are rarely any major objections when it comes to the design. The client has already agreed on the brief, the key narrative, and the visual idea. It's up to us as the designers to translate that into something visual.

We come up with many concepts during our process, but we only present one idea. Our clients know this from the beginning, and it's rare when they want to pay extra for several ideas. We think that's smart: we're the experts, and it's our job to choose the visual direction. We've learned that it's better to show one great idea than three, because presenting

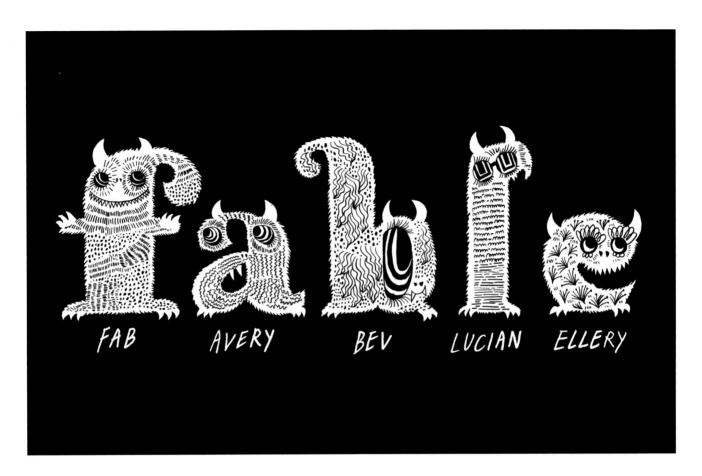

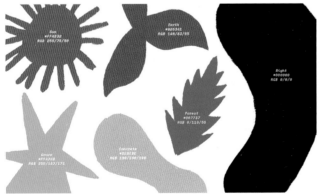

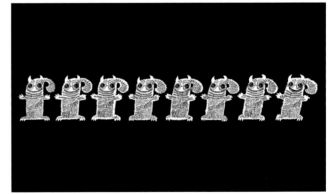

Gender-neutral character names add depth to the identity.

a range will only confuse the client, and it might result in them wanting to combine pieces from each, which is never good.

If a client doesn't accept the idea we present, we have to take a step back to determine where the problem lies. Perhaps we misinterpreted the client's expectations. Or maybe there was internal resistance in the client's company. It's usually that we took the concept too far toward the extreme. It's our opinion that differentiation is always interesting, so we often try to move brands toward something that hasn't previously been done, and people are sometimes afraid of the unknown. Everyone loves change—except when it comes to themselves. For us, it's rare that a client doesn't like the idea, and after the presentation the discussion is mostly about small details.

Identity guidelines

The creation of a guidelines document depends on the client's internal structure. Some clients have an in-house design team that is experienced with reading visual manuals, whereas some have no experience whatsoever and need to have very clear rules on how to apply the visual elements.

All our identity projects result in guidelines of some form. Sometimes it's just a couple of slides in a PDF. Other times, it's a ninety-page PDF. Occasionally we'll create a visual guidelines website. It's unnecessary to make the guidelines more complex than they have to be.

Clients with an in-house team need to understand a few things about the new visual identity, such as what we're trying to achieve, what we're trying to communicate, and why that's relevant for the brand. One way to facilitate this is through a workshop where we meet with the staff at a company and take them through our thinking for all the various identity elements.

Environmental friendliness

We do as much as we possibly can to reduce our carbon footprint. One way is by using printers as close to the final destination as possible. Sweden has a lot of good paper stockers, so we rarely ship paper from other countries. We also use bike couriers, and we travel to client meetings by bike or public transport.

Finding your first clients

When we started in business, we made hundreds of cold calls to potential clients, but that rarely resulted in anything. Most of our clients come through friends or personal connections. Our first client came through a friend who started working with a small furniture company, Essem Design, and it turned out they needed a new website. Everything just spiraled from there.

Key points

Five important client questions to address in the design brief include: What are we going to do? Who are we speaking to? What is our core message? What feeling(s) do we want to communicate? What should the overall result be?

Take a close look at your client's competitors, because moving in the opposite direction will always help with differentiation.

As designers, we're the experts, and it's our job to set the visual direction, so don't feel you need to present more than one idea.

Robot Food

Leeds
www.robot-food.com

Project: Vocation

Vocation is a Yorkshire, England–based craft brewery whose bold, distinctive beers enjoy huge success in retailers, bars, and restaurants nationwide, and beyond.

Coaster design

Most of our clients approach us after seeing our work on our website, on Behance, or in the press. This was the case with John Hickling, founder and head brewer at Vocation. At the time, it felt like kismet as we'd been wanting to work on a beer brand and he needed a visual identity for his new brewery.

Initial questions

First, we asked John about his story. He told us about quitting his previous career in banking and starting a brewery in which he ultimately sold his shares. After taking a year off, he was ready and prepared to brew the kind of beers he wanted to drink—heavy-hitting, hop-forward, American-style ales. We found his passion and vision compelling. So compelling, in fact, that when he told us he wanted to name the business "Brewery on the Hill," it wasn't so much a question of "Why?" but rather, a definitive "No," as we knew we could come up with something much more fitting and enduring.

As we've grown, we've developed the early stage of projects to include full immersion and stakeholder interviews. The questions we ask our clients vary depending on the project, but ultimately, what's most important is to obtain a good overall view of the business and gauge its ambition from different perspectives.

The design brief

We have a briefing template that we email to clients to fill out. In it, we aim to discover the background of a project; what the client sees as the opportunity, the target consumer, and competitive landscape; how they are perceived now and how they want to be perceived; and, ultimately, what the tasks and deliverables are. This is just the first step. The answers lead to further questions to fully develop the brief, helping us to understand client objectives and reveal specific areas we can improve on. Client perceptions of their brand can often be very different than those of others, so it's important that designers and clients work as partners to be sure about which areas of the branding do and don't need development.

The deliverables

Initially the Vocation brief was pretty comprehensive: a brand identity, bottle label design, pump clips, and potential merchandise. The design for the cans followed soon after. We still work with Vocation today on many exciting extensions, including designs for new beer styles and limited editions. Most recently, we worked on Vocation & Co., a taproom and kitchen based in its hometown of Hebden Bridge in Yorkshire.

Terms and conditions

Our terms and conditions (T&C) are on our website and, when it comes to having clients agree to them, an email confirmation will do the trick.

The nature of our working relationships means that we've never had to refer our clients back to the terms, but it's good to have them in place should we need them. We go through a standard process prior to any project that includes gathering full account details so we're always aware of who's in charge and responsible for payment. It's a degree of professionalism that any client would expect.

We require a percentage deposit before we start work. We ask this of every client as a commitment to see the project through together. We won't provide free pitching or concept work because our ideas are our currency, and you should never devalue your currency.

The core Vocation range

We have had issues getting paid, but they're not something we dwell on. In the past, personnel changes or a loss of commercial opportunity for the client have led to payment delays. That's why your T&C is so important.

Knowing what to charge

In our early days of business, we obtained various agency quotes and used them as starting points. We're always honing and refining our process, which we consider a work in progress that should constantly be revisited.

We're always honing and refining our process, which we consider a work in progress that should constantly be revisited.

Today we establish the brief first, so we know exactly what's expected. Then we base all our project quotes on the hourly costs of the relevant team members, and the estimated time for completion. Time is money, and although our approach is bespoke, we draw upon past experience to judge how long the work might take. A project like this would usually last twelve to sixteen weeks. Vocation was at the shorter end of that time frame. Quotes are agreed on in advance, with any additions to the scope also quoted for and agreed upon before they begin.

As Vocation was a start-up, John had a low budget expectation. We explained that it would cost considerably more to do the job properly, but he was concerned with cash flow. We offered flexibility in our usual fee structure because we were confident that John would reach his goals, so our initial agreement was a payment structure that worked for him, including a first-year, target-related bonus. We also knew what this project could mean for our portfolio, so there was an element of self-interest. John was happy for us to take the lead on the creative aspect because we are essentially Vocation's target market. It really was a win-win situation.

On client negotiation

Many factors influence whether we can negotiate. As said previously, we consider what kind of an opportunity a project presents for our portfolio, as we did with Vocation, and we also look at the business itself, gauging the expectations and ambitions of the client. We work with people and projects that we believe in so, on occasion, we'll consider reducing our fees in return for a stake in the business. Negotiation works best when you have honesty and trust on both sides.

Payment

We request an up-front percentage of the fee for any project with a new client and then invoice on

The Pilsner range

completion of each stage, offering thirty days' credit. If it's a smaller project, we might wait and invoice the remainder at the end.

We accept almost any form of payment and typically do our best to accommodate our clients. The only time we might try to steer them in a different direction is if the payment method might incur a considerable fee.

The payment process doesn't differ too much with overseas clients. Sometimes we'll charge in a different currency to make it easier for clients to understand the cost implications. You win some and lose some with exchange rates, but we see any loss as a business cost rather than a reduction in fee.

Conducting research

Our process is quite flexible, but it usually follows the same staged approach. For a new brand such as Vocation, we'll start with full immersion followed by research and category audits. This then feeds into a workshop that helps to define the essence of the brand—its values, mission, and tone of voice. The outcome of the workshop is distilled into a "brand bible" that informs a naming workshop (if required) and our design strategy and proposition process—research, analyze, and define, or RAD.

The key to every project is understanding the motivations of the target consumer. We look to fill the gaps in the category we're operating in, but try to avoid getting caught up in the confines of its semiotics or crafting an identity that's similar to what else is out there. Once we understand the type of person we're targeting, we can then look at and draw from other categories and successful brands that they engage with. By learning from their nuances, e.g., the way the other brands look

and communicate, you can create something that resonates with the consumer from day one. This is especially important for start-up brands.

The key to every project is understanding the motivations of the target consumer.

Merging strategy and design

The point where strategy meets design is our own internal process, RAD. It's difficult to articulate the "how" because it's different with every project. For Vocation, our aim was to create distinction by ignoring what had come before in craft beer design and making the beer and its flavor the hero above anything else. It's what felt right. Strategy is the DNA of every brand—once you've nailed that, design is the easy bit.

When to stop experimenting

We plan the amount of time we'll need to develop the concept and try to stick to it. In the design process, however, you can sometimes struggle to reach the right solution within the allocated time frame, especially when creating something completely new. In those instances, we won't stop our concept work until we get it just right. Likewise, if we still have time

Clothing, kegs, and packaging were other parts of the project.

left but are confident that what we've come up with truly fulfills the brief, then we'll move forward. The quality of the creative work is the most important part of the process and often comes down to intuition.

Everybody has their own way of dealing with creative block. If we ever find it particularly challenging to generate ideas, then generally, it's best to just get up and go somewhere—for a walk or a coffee. You can be influenced by something you see, hear, or randomly think of, and suddenly you have another direction.

Copyright and trademarking
We recommend an intellectual property lawyer to our clients to trademark the identities we create in order to prevent copycats. With Vocation, there have been quite a few "renditions" of our creative work, both inside and outside the beer, wine, and spirits category. Ultimately, it's up to the client to take legal action against any commercial threat. For us, we just see it as a compliment, although there was one T-shirt seller who we contacted just because of how brazen the Vocation rip-off was. The seller apologized and stopped immediately.

As an agency, we've never had to rule out any design because of similarities with something else. Everyone on the team is aware that you can borrow but never directly copy a design. That's a matter of pride, in addition to legality.

Presenting the work
The whole sequence is a filtering process. After strategy and predesign, we usually create two or three mood boards with visual and verbal propositions. We present these to the client for discussion.

We'll narrow them down to one or two and base the concept work on them. This means that what the client sees afterward are different visual interpretations of a proposition that everyone has approved.

Clients will know from the outset that we typically present three to five design options. You need to provide variations to explore the design. We use the concepts to gauge how far the client is comfortable in stretching the level of creativity used in the outcome. They also help us explore different approaches to communication hierarchy, iconography, and photographic style.

We don't try to steer anyone toward a specific design direction, even though we usually have our own preference. We're happy to share our thoughts prior to hearing client feedback. If there are any words that help to sway the decision, "Boom," tends to do the job.

We'll photograph as many elements as we can so that designs can be comped onto something that looks closest to the real deal. Photography has a much nicer quality than digital mock-ups and provides a more accurate representation. It makes such a difference when the client is reviewing our work.

The avoidance of micromanaging
After both parties agree on the design brief, we create a list with the client of evaluation criteria based on the project's objectives. We'll go back to it during the concept presentation to keep everything on track. It helps to keep the focus on meeting consumer needs rather than the individual tastes of the client.

Sometimes, due to the hierarchy in a business, the person making the final decision isn't the same person who briefed the project, so it's possible that

The Vocation & Co. taproom and kitchen,
in Hebden Bridge, Yorkshire, England

previously agreed-on objectives can change. This isn't always a bad thing—sometimes it takes a fresh set of eyes to help identify a new or different problem that needs solving.

Developing guidelines

Not every project needs a style guide because we're often responsible for the rollout. If a client requests one, we make sure to cover every eventuality so that brand consistency is retained regardless of who works from the guidelines.

When we provide a style guide, we supply it in whichever format the client prefers—most of the time it's a PDF, but we've also produced printed versions in a style that physically feels like it belongs to the brand.

At the beginning of our client discussions, we always ask for, and cost in, the ability to see and sign off on any design before it's released. We don't want any work that has our name attached to it compromised. We like to think of ourselves as brand guardians, so that even after a project is finished, we'll get in touch with the client if we spot an execution that doesn't feel right. The strength and consistency of the brand are all that matter.

Measuring success

We're always keen to learn of statistics that demonstrate how our design helps clients achieve their goals. It's important for our credibility and our own reassurance that what we do actually makes a difference.

Usually we'll do this by calling the client or going to an official debriefing. For Vocation, we made a video and interviewed John about his experience. He talked about the success that he and the team had achieved in the first year, and even called us

Vocation's "fifth Beatle." That meant a lot. Vocation is now stocked in most major supermarkets as well as trendy bars and liquor stores that also sell its craft contemporaries.

Good design can deliver a compelling aesthetic, but great design delivers on objectives and drives growth. There's nothing better than knowing you've taken a start-up, or a brand in decline, and made it engaging enough to succeed.

Finding your first clients

Create demand by banging your own drum. Robot Food was founded by two people—Simon Forster, who had no experience, and his friend from art school, Mike Shaw, who had worked as a designer in an agency. We couldn't show any of Mike's previous work, so we made up our own creative concepts and promoted them as if they were real. We were featured on blogs and in the press and, soon after, the real work started coming in.

Key points

Once you understand the audience you're targeting, you can then pull potential ideas from other brands they engage with (not necessarily competing brands).

You can help to take the subjectivity out of your design presentation by using a list of evaluation criteria that's previously agreed upon with the client.

Good design can deliver a compelling aesthetic, but great design delivers on objectives and drives growth.

Together Design

London
www.togetherdesign.co.uk

Project: Pearson

Pearson refers to itself as the world's leading learning company, with revenues of £5 billion ($6.5 billion) and more than 30,000 employees in 80 countries worldwide. In 2015, it began the transition from educational print publisher to digital and service-oriented learning business, and from corporate holding company to customer-facing brand.

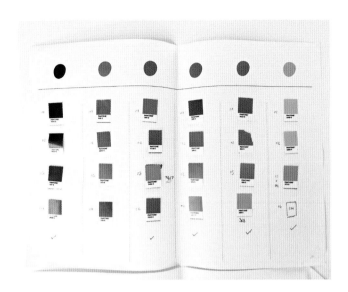

Palette and pattern experimentation

We were introduced to Pearson by a small rabbit or, more accurately, someone whom we had worked with on the Peter Rabbit licensing guidelines! This is typical for us, as the vast majority of our clients come through referrals and recommendations. We find these new conversations are more positive and open because the people we're meeting are already familiar with our business and what they can expect from us.

Pearson came to us with a good idea of what they wanted, but not with a detailed brief, which is also typical. We worked together to understand the challenges they faced and possible solutions, as well as the best approach for doing so.

Pearson initially felt they needed guidelines to help implement and bring together a new global visual identity. We realized from the first meeting that we were going to need a great deal of strategic input so the identity guidance didn't simply revolve around visually aligning the overarching branding. Our work also needed to underpin the strategic business objectives, informing the entire product and service portfolio with a solution that was both broad and deep.

Initial questions

It's key to understand where the brief is coming from, the challenge it seeks to address, how success will be measured, who'll be involved (internally and externally), the sign-off process, as well as geographical spread, timings, and budgets. Pearson is more complicated than most organizations, so we had a lot of questions about the business structure in order to understand the breadth of use for the visual identity.

These types of questions also give us insight into the client's perception of their challenges and where the project sits among the company's overall priorities. The answers help us to manage expectations and, most important, identify areas that are unclear or haven't yet been considered. This is where we can help refine the brief and avoid foreseeable obstacles in the future.

It's key to understand where the brief is coming from, the challenge it seeks to address, and how success will be measured.

Our first exploratory meeting brought up many questions about the overarching brand model, the company structure, the impact of the company reorganization, naming conventions or rules, and the project structure that might be needed for their internal team, our team, and our working

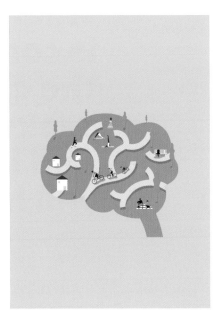

Brand illustrations by (clockwise from top left) Tang Yau Hoong,
Lauren Rolwing, Ben Wiseman, Lauren Rolwing, Lauren Rolwing,
Davide Bonazzi

relationship. This led to establishing dedicated project teams from Together Design and Pearson, as well as subteams and independent collaborators to handle specific areas.

One of our first tasks was to organize weekly face-to-face meetings with the core client team and weekly calls with extended teams to ensure clear and timely communication and the most effective use of resources. We initially wondered whether weekly meetings might be overkill—too much talking, not enough doing—but we could never have achieved the identity launch date without them. Each week we showed progress on multiple fronts, and the instant feedback and decision-making meant we could move quickly ahead. It also meant that decisions were made together and everyone was there to argue their point if needed.

The deliverables

To start with, the only requested deliverable was visual identity guidelines. The client had written a rough idea of content on one sheet of paper. But we then worked out that marketing assets (e.g., exhibition stands) hadn't yet been created and design rules hadn't been set or tested. So, we had to step back to understand the practical and emotional criteria for everything we would produce and the full context of how the guide would be used. As the scale of the task became apparent, our work list grew enormously.

We launched Pearson's new branding six months later. During the three years we worked together, we delivered Pearson's overarching brand model, rolled out its global identity, and developed a framework showing the relationships and functions of the more than 2,500 products and services in their extensive portfolio. We've delivered thousands of pages of guidance, from core colors, logo creation, and accessibility, to trade shows, campaigns, and merchandise. We've also rebranded multiple offerings in their portfolio—covering everything from an e-library in India to a language school in Brazil to a publisher in Germany. We've briefed student award programs, developed a library of illustrations and pictograms for global use, and established the direction for the crowdsourced photographic library. We've been involved in developing brand management tools for internal training (both on- and offline), and we've carried out external brand engagement and training activities.

Before receiving payment

With all our projects, we do a lot of research and thinking before we meet a client. This means we can have a detailed conversation about the potential project and demonstrate the level of detail that we take great pride in. Once the project and costs have been agreed on, we typically work out a payment program—often divided equally over the project length and billed monthly in arrears. We commence work after the client agrees to the scope of work and fees.

We occasionally work in countries where payment can be much slower than average or where laws are different, such as China or Russia. In such cases, it's standard practice to ask for 50 percent of the fee in advance. This would also be true for projects that have a very quick turnaround or that need us to cover out-of-pocket external expenses on the client's behalf.

Setting terms and conditions

We provide fairly standard terms and conditions, covering confidentiality, intellectual property (IP)

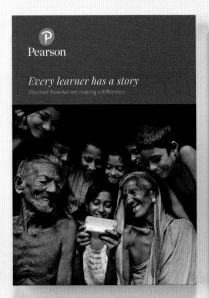

Every learner has a story
Discover how we are making a difference

Each of us can make a world of difference

Find out how our products transform learners' lives

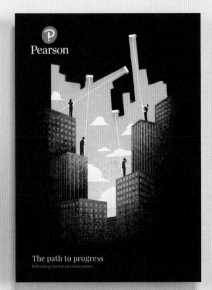

The path to progress
Rethinking the future of education

Fuel your curiosity and *spark* your imagination

A world of learning is *just a click away*

Today, tomorrow, and the future

Printed launch and marketing collateral

ownership, and payment terms. Our proposal, to which the client agrees before work commences, states, "Agreeing to this proposal is an agreement to our standard terms and conditions." With larger clients, there may also be a non-disclosure agreement or contract to sign.

Once or twice in the past, a client has wanted full IP rights to the work produced, which isn't standard in our terms. In that case, we would negotiate the agreement before any work begins.

In almost fifteen years of business, we've only once had to get legal help for procuring payment. We had to remind a client via our lawyers that they didn't have permission to use our design work until our final bill was settled. As they'd already put the logo on their website, payment quickly followed.

Ultimately when it comes to a smooth working relationship, it's the amount of detail in the proposal, the time line, and the early discussions that helps to manage expectations and prevent misunderstandings.

Knowing what to charge

We have standard studio rates for each of our employees, depending on what they do and their level of seniority. We assemble our fees according to the time required to deliver the specific task. Our years of experience help us to determine the costs needed to complete a project. We're very transparent with clients; we discuss daily rates and project fees in detail so they work with us to stick to the agreed budget.

We prepare all our project costs in the same way, based on the time we'll spend. We don't change our daily rate for different clients, but our approach is

flexible. Different client teams can provide more or less project support, so we're generally able to find an approach and a fee to accommodate most budgets.

Occasionally, and only if appropriate, we deliver a "menu" style proposal that enables clients on a more limited budget to pick and choose the items they'd most like to prioritize—those they can't deliver themselves. Reducing the number of creative concepts, say from three to two, can also help reduce the time required.

It's the amount of detail in the proposal, the time line, and the early discussions that helps to manage expectations.

Our fees and costs fall in the middle of industry standards and are always open to negotiation. If the project scope can be reduced, our fees will be reduced.

We analyze past projects to ensure that our cost estimates are accurate. We review our rates annually

Various extensions of the visual identity

with our financial advisor and typically raise them every few years depending on industry standards and outgoing costs. We're eager to remain as competitive as possible and never want to price ourselves out of the sectors we're most passionate about.

We invoice in British pounds sterling and typically absorb any variation in exchange rates between invoicing and payment. We don't send receipts, and WorkflowMax is our timesheet, account management, and billing system. We accept payment by bank transfer, check (for nostalgic reasons), and occasionally, chocolate!

Estimating the project time frame

The best indicator for assessing the time needed to deliver a task is our experience. We draw on it regularly. We won't accept a task if we feel that the budget doesn't allow for the time needed. The growth and health of our business relies on referrals and recommendations, and we get these because our clients are happy and because they achieve success with help from the work we deliver. If we embark on a project feeling disgruntled about fees, sensing a lack of respect or trust in what we do, it's a surefire path to disappointing results.

With the Pearson project, the initial visual identity was six months in the making, a super quick turnaround for the level of detail we had to go into—we delivered the one hundred and forty–page branding guide (translated into four languages) on time, along with a large amount of launch and support material. Since then, our work with Pearson has continued, and, three years later, we're still delivering a number of projects to them each month.

Conducting research and defining the strategy

Pearson is a global brand with thirty thousand employees, so change at this level requires a vast amount of engagement and internal research. During our time on the project, we carried out more than one hundred qualitative interviews and dozens of workshops with various client teams around the world. Conducting brand, customer, and competitor audits, as well as benchmarking, are a standard approach for us, and form a part of most projects, including Pearson.

You're going in blind without having a well-researched and sense-checked understanding of your clients' history, culture, objectives, and ongoing requirements. Every single detail of Pearson's visual identity had rock-solid criteria behind its reason for being. Strategy means different things to different people and is a word that's often used without a helpful prefix. To us it means careful planning and making decisions backed up by fact and insight. There are many available techniques to determine fact and insight. We have long conversations with the client to figure out the best approach— it may be a combination of qualitative interviews, workshops, desk research, and more—to deepen our understanding of their challenges and opportunities.

The creative brief

We put the brief in place following research and workshops. This is not to say that we don't have a defined project brief already in place. The project brief and creative brief are often very different, with the former being defined before our proposal, fees, and working terms have been signed off on. The latter is

Branded stands and marketing material
for events and trade shows

defined collaboratively, usually after the first research stage. It can come in many different formats, such as a mood board that we've used for stimulus in a workshop or research phase. It might be a summary as part of a positioning statement. It might be a written list of emotive ambitions, such as "How do we want our audience to feel?" It could be practical and technical requirements. It could be all of these.

Merging strategy and design

Practically speaking, we hold a creative workshop when we enter the creative phase of a project to understand the brand model, priority customers, competitive positioning, overarching proposition, and core values and attributes. These strategic pillars help to inform our selection of colors, fonts, photographic styling, and illustration. Is the brand high-end or low-end? Is it warm or cool? Is it more male or female or gender neutral? Is there a sense of history and heritage? Is it traditional or about the future? The answers to all these questions give a great sense of the general creative direction.

Copyright and trademarking

Copyright infringement can, and does, happen all the time. It's often only at the point of global legal searches that you become aware of conflicts or problems, and that's another reason to do your research well.

We frequently work with IP lawyers, and during the Pearson project, we were in regular contact with their global legal team. Trademark registration, especially for global brands, is a complex, time-consuming, and costly affair that involves many factors to consider—the name, visual identity, short forms, icons, and third-party partnerships. At nearly

every turn, there's an opportunity for a brand to build positive equity, but equally, to be negatively affected by misrepresentation.

A good understanding of IP law is also a way to find cost reductions for a client. By using free typefaces, we instantly made a huge saving for Pearson's font library.

Presenting the work

We tend to start our design process by developing mood boards, bringing different design routes to life through a series of found images, words, colors, and textures. This gives clients an impression of our direction and us an opportunity to get initial feedback to refine our creative approach before we get stuck into the design of unique elements. Our name is Together Design because we believe in collaboration, so we would never disappear for a month and then present a client with one refined and perfect solution—the solution is always an ongoing discussion.

We generally look at two or three routes, depending on what's relevant, and the number is agreed on with the client in advance. Each direction isn't a stab in the dark, but rather a properly explored, interrogated, and refined brief that we're working to. The mood board phase ensures our routes are validated with the client team. It's unnecessary to develop more than three avenues if you're working to a planned and agreed-on set of success criteria.

We don't often have a favorite direction. The trick is not to present something you'd be disappointed with. Our different routes emphasize various areas of the brief, and each will have a clear rationale that's directly linked to the brand model, the brief, and all our earlier discussions. On the occasion when

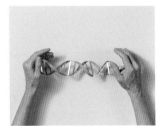

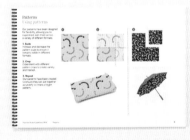

Pearson Design Story video and brand guidelines

we do have a preferred route and, if asked for our preference, we offer our recommendations in an objective manner.

Feedback on our presentations is also objective, rational, and helpful to achieve a successful design solution. That's because the criteria for judging the design is clear and agreed on up front and we all understand the business objectives and questions that our work needs to answer. One person's favorite color will never be reflective of one organization's entire audience.

Client involvement at every step of the way in defining the strategy means there aren't many surprises when showing the work. If clients are engaged and involved, then they have cocreated. If they have cocreated, then they co-own. If they co-own, they don't reject the end result. That's not to say we haven't had clients who were very hard to please or who changed the brief along the way. This happens, and we work through it together. In such cases where a brief has changed and needs to be rewritten, we'd ask for agreement on additional fees.

Brand guidelines

Providing guidance rather than guidelines is a positive move. There are rules and guardrails for sure, but they're balanced with inspiration and encouragement. Our job is to empower client teams, giving them the tools to manage and develop their own brands. Identity guidelines that delight clients (and other agencies they might work with) prove to be more useful, with a much longer lifespan. Effective guidelines must be easy to use, technically perfect, and interesting to look at and read. For this project,

we produced seventeen separate guideline documents for Pearson's master brand visual identity, and dozens of other guidelines for our rebranding of their various products and services.

Our guidelines tend to be PDFs, interactive or not. Some clients have sophisticated asset management systems that we need to align with or create, while, with others, it's a simple FTP link and the job's done.

Most sizeable identity projects need guidelines at the end to record the thinking and design decisions, but some smaller ones don't. Smaller client teams may need training more than guidelines.

Effective identity guidelines must be easy to use, technically perfect, and interesting to look at and read.

When ensuring that the work we create ends up "on the street," it's back to the cocreate idea. If our clients have been with us on the journey, then they're even more passionate about great implementation than we are, and we usually work hand in hand when

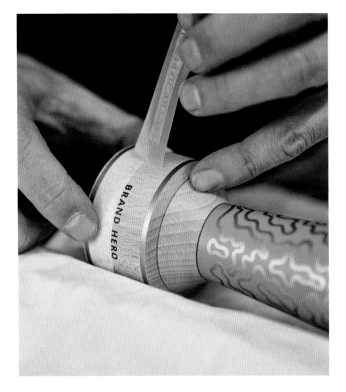

The custom-made Brand Hero award for Pearson employees

planning the launch and rollout. With Pearson, we were involved in internal training and developing online training, and we've been part of the brand help desk team and hosted design forums to share our thinking and hear from Pearson designers around the world. In projects where there is no formal ongoing relationship, we offer a check-in period to see how the materials are shaping up.

Measuring success

There are many ways to check in, both formally and informally. Once a client, always a friend—that's what we hope for, anyway. We tend to see people informally and hear how things are going. We also get in touch with a client if we publish a case study of the work, such as on our website, and we always ask about results at that point.

We also enter (and are sometimes lucky enough to win) a fair number of design award competitions. The process of preparing for awards means touching base with clients and finding out how our work has affected their business, how implementation has gone, and where they want to take it.

Finding your first clients

As mentioned, we've been lucky to grow our business mostly through referrals and recommendations, and we don't do a great deal of regular, organized marketing activity. That said, we do a huge amount to encourage positive word of mouth. We regularly keep in touch with our clients, business friends, and collaborators through newsletters, trend reports, social media, and even Valentine's Day mailers.

Our experience suggests that clients appreciate communication that adds value to their business and delivers insight into their markets and customers. Clients are targeted by service providers all the time and you need to find a way of adding something new to the conversation. We also have a huge party every year to bring people together, and we run our own online shop, which is another fun excuse to keep in contact with people. For anyone starting up, our advice is that your friends can become clients, and your clients can become friends.

Environmental friendliness

From our choice of printing paper to our electricity supplier, we choose environmentally friendly suppliers wherever possible. We try to be equally thoughtful in our client work, which is especially important, challenging, and exciting when it comes to packaging projects. We're always thinking of the three "r's"—reduce, recycle, and reuse.

Key points

Is the brand high-end or low-end? Is it warm or cool? Is it analytical or emotional? Friendly or aloof? Is there a sense of history and heritage? Is it traditional or about the future? The answers to all these questions give a great sense of the general creative direction.

Never present something you'd be disappointed in the client choosing.

Your friends can become clients, and your clients can become friends.

grain®

Believe in®

Exeter + Mono
www.believein.net

Project: Grain

Grain was founded in 2017 and builds hyperfast broadband networks for housing developments across the United Kingdom.

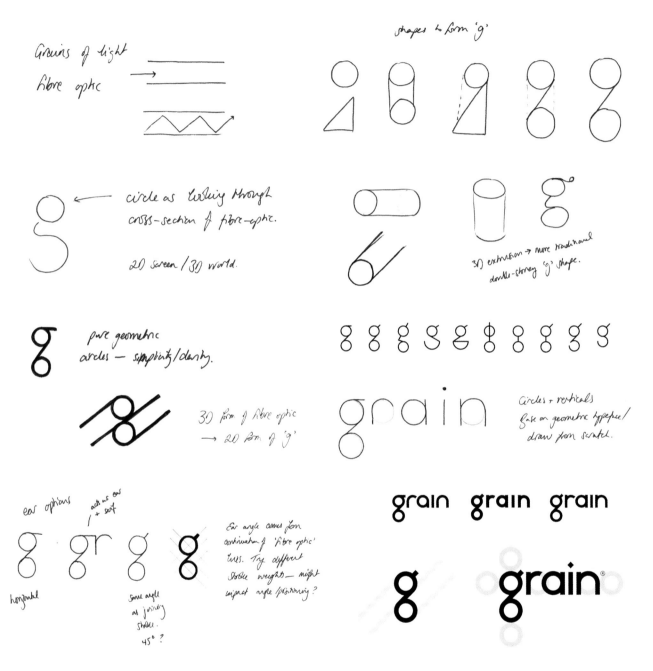

Grains of light
fibre optic

shapes to form 'g'

circle as looking through
cross-section of fibre-optic.

2D screen / 3D world.

3D extrusion → more traditional
double-storey 'g' shape.

pure geometric
circles — simplicity/clarity.

3D form of fibre optic
→ 2D form of 'g'

grain

Circles + verticals
Base on geometric typeface/
draw from scratch.

ear options

act as ear
+ serif

gr

horizontal

same angle
as joining
stroke.
45°?

Ear angle comes from
continuation of 'fibre optic'
lines. Try different
stroke weights — might
impact angle/positioning?

grain   grain   grain

g   grain®

Wordmark and monogram sketches and development

The company is a joint venture between a London-based property development client of ours and a telecom company based in the northwest. Our client asked us to present our approach, and the joint venture partner invited their preferred agency to do the same.

New client relationships usually begin in one of three ways: 1) some people see our work in a publication or online and get in touch, 2) others contact us following a recommendation from someone they trust, or 3) we approach someone to suggest how we might help them. Our aim is to build strong relationships with clients who will stay with us because of the level of service, depth of thought, and quality of outcome that we have provided.

Initial questions

The client was clear on what the business needed to do but had little sense of how that might feel from a customer's perspective. With every new client, our goal is to give them an understanding of what it's like to work with us and earn their confidence in our approach and the quality of our advice. This means the research and strategy work starts before we've been hired. There are fundamental questions that apply to most projects, but it's our ability to explore a given answer that adds depth to the understanding.

Project deliverables

The project consisted of limited research, brand strategy, name development (including intellectual property protection), and the core identity and wider identity system (including color, typography, imagery, tone of voice, and basic guidelines). The launch applications included an initial "starter" website and a basic suite of printed materials.

Tasks before receiving payment

The first conversation with a potential client is technically research, and any advice you give contributes toward the development of a strategy. There's no hard line between selling and doing, as one flows naturally into the other. We don't do speculative design work because it's bad for the client. Asking them to form a meaningful opinion on the basis of some hastily assembled visuals is not fair to them, and they deserve better from us.

Speculative design work is bad for the client. They deserve better from us.

Terms and conditions

Terms of business are there as a last resort, as they're often not read (think of iTunes's fifty-six pages of legal terms that must be agreed to before using the software). It's how you communicate throughout the job that establishes expectations.

Every project starts with a set of assumptions that need to be worked through so we can plot an ideal path to the desired result. This means that having a fixed view of what should happen is usually unrealistic.

Every project flows within a framework that acts as scaffolding. We ensure the client understands the various stages and recognizes that recommendations from each stage will affect the work to follow.

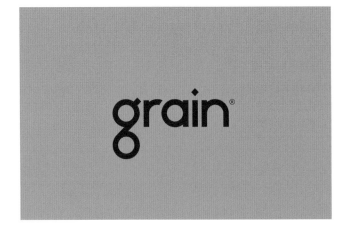

Grain wordmark with supporting shapes

So with a framework providing structure, an ability to respond along the way, and a meticulous approach to documenting decisions, we protect ourselves and the client and hopefully avoid any awkward conversations or confusion.

We allow clients to accept our terms via email. We are currently investigating an alternative that includes a digital signature, but that's more for the customer experience than for any legal security.

Lessons learned

We learned some hard lessons in the early days, including one involving a client who went bust not once, but twice. We worked with them again in the hope of recouping some of the money we lost the first time around, and got stung again. Often your gut will have a pretty clear idea of how a situation might play out, so ignore it at your peril.

We have threatened to bring in our lawyers a couple of times but managed to resolve the situations before they were needed. The most important things you can do to avoid similar situations are to communicate effectively and keep good records. It's always better to spend a few hours spelling out why the client's assumptions are incorrect and backing that up with evidence than resorting to litigation. When a communication trail is vague or incomplete, you open up the possibility of gifting the client an amount of money that's rightfully yours.

Knowing what to charge

After we define what the client needs, we provide an estimate that's calculated on the amount of work required and its anticipated value. For a charity or micro-business, we may apply a slightly lower rate, giving us the time we need at a price they can hopefully afford. Bigger clients pay more, as there is typically more time and involvement required, plus a greater focus on minimizing risk.

If budgets are an issue, we may look for ways to limit the project scope or deliverables, always making sure the client understands what's not included. We've found that our day rates are often equal to, or cheaper than, those of other agencies, but we have a more realistic sense of how much time is needed to do the job properly.

Fees for the Grain project totaled slightly more than £60,000 ($77,000), including the launch applications. This amount was split into £25,000 ($32,000) for the initial brand development (research, strategy, name, and identity system) and just over £35,000 ($45,000) for the launch applications.

We assign a cost to each project stage, which allows for flexibility in the final price as the client can prioritize certain elements over others. It's not a menu of options, and sacrificing certain work might increase costs elsewhere, so we try to understand the client's budget and help them to spend it in the most sensible way. There will always be an amount we can't drop below.

Our pricing strategy has evolved around the principle that a realistic and grownup discussion about the work involved will lead to a position that's suitable for everyone. Other methods might maximize fees more effectively, but we feel that ours puts the relationship on the right footing, and we hope that our clients appreciate this more straightforward approach.

When there's a negotiation, we try to be clear about what's up for discussion and what's not. Some clients can't discuss an opportunity without trying to secure a deal of some kind. We won't let a client pick and choose, but we may propose a way to limit

A sample of stock photography (left) and the resulting images
with brand treatment (right)

the scope of the work in order to deliver a budget reduction. Over-servicing clients is common, so we try to determine costs in a way that safeguards the quality of our work without giving too much away.

Estimating the time frame

The timetable is based on the amount of work involved, the client's commercial requirements, and our current workload. We're pretty good at sticking to our time estimates, and delays more commonly arise on the client side.

For Grain, we plotted a full timetable for all stages to meet the client's desired launch date. Our timetables include not only the amount of time we require, but also how much time we give a client to respond. The stage that ran over was name development, and that's pretty common. From start to finish, the brand development took eighteen weeks (two more weeks than planned), while the launch applications followed six weeks after that.

Handling payment

Payment terms vary by client, depending on their history and perceived risk. For new clients, we invoice an agreed-on percentage in advance and then invoice each stage upon completion.

For many, often larger clients, the initial up-front invoice will give us the confidence to extend credit terms (usually thirty days). For others, we may request trade references from existing suppliers, otherwise we may continue invoicing in advance until a track record of reliable payment is established. We rarely use an external credit scoring agency, but credit is not automatically given.

If a delay occurs outside our control, then we invoice work up to date. Over the years, we've grown more robust in the way we approach credit control and chasing payment. You should never be afraid of asking a client to uphold their side of the bargain, just as they expect you to uphold yours.

Invoices are invariably settled by electronic bank transfer. Clients are free to pay us in other ways, but they tend not to.

Research

With Grain, we were creating a new brand from scratch, so it wasn't about how we could do things better, but how we could do things at all. This involved lots of desk research into the sector, understanding and defining the customer experience, plus customer profiling. Research was limited because of budget constraints, but it's always a significant part of how we work. We had no existing customers to talk to, but carried out interviews with industry contacts.

Strategy

Strategy underpins any good design, and without it, you could be designing anything. The result might look lovely, but it won't mean much. For a brand, strategy is more than just a brief. It's the meaning that a brand carries and it provides reasons for everything that it chooses to do (or not do). The best brands measure their progress against the ideas contained within the strategy.

Through the project stages

Each stage includes an output, a document that must be signed off on before we can start on the next stage. The document varies, depending on the stage. A brand strategy output, for example, is usually as simple as a single page that explains the approach. The client replies to our email that has the document

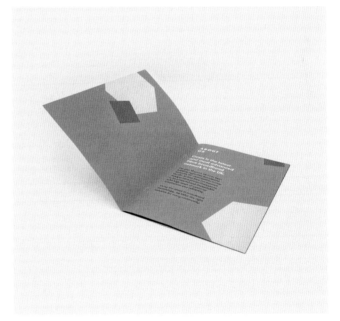

Promotional booklet with brand palette and type

attached and confirms they agree and are happy for us to proceed to the next stage.

You can't develop a strategy without the research, and the strategy is needed for the name development, and so on. You can assume everyone's happy, but if you develop work on the basis of that assumption, don't be surprised if the client objects at some point and forces you to go backward.

From strategy to design
The strategy always pushes the design in a certain direction. Brand archetypes carry strong visual connotations, e.g., an Outlaw will present itself in a more irreverent way than a Ruler brand. If the strategy defines a customer experience, then the resulting feelings will be expressed in the visual treatment. Whether it's color, tone of voice, imagery, or typography, every aspect of the design should relate to the strategy.

Grain's wordmark is intentionally very simple. It starts from a technical beginning, but expresses itself in a distinctly human way. The supporting animations and illustrations show people at play in a digital world. The color palette adds a vibrant energy, with bold shapes that can play at varying scales. The copy is crisp and smart, with a touch of wit, but never trying too hard.

Generating ideas
Everyone has a different approach for coming up with ideas; you have to find which way works for you. Some people employ techniques such as "Thinkertoys" to help them consider the brief from as many different vantage points as possible. Others like to generate elaborate mind maps, i.e., organizational diagrams. Some people go for a walk with a voice recorder and

talk to themselves. Others dive straight into sketching and scribbling. For most of us, it's about working through the obvious stuff in search of a jumping-off point to somewhere more interesting.

Avoiding copyright infringement
There are databases of icons and symbols that you can search, but they're pretty unreliable. Unfortunately, the best way to find a pre-existing mark is to post it online and wait for someone to recognize it. We use tools such as Google Images and TinEye to help identify conflicting designs. Most designers have thrown out winning concepts because of something that looks too similar, and we're certainly no different.

Much of our work, such as that for Grain, includes developing a brand name. As a process, it is fraught with danger, and managing expectations is vital. Although we're happy to present a single identity concept, we can't do the same thing with naming unless our client is happy to place all their trust (and the ultimate decision) in our hands.

Names are so emotive, and they need to be presented with as little design as possible, which has a major effect on how they're perceived. We usually present a shortlist of ten to twelve options, aiming for three or four to be carried through for thorough checking.

We wanted Grain to stand out in a crowded market as doing something different, and that began with the name. Most broadband firms rely on ideas of speed, high tech, and whooshing graphics, but our strategy demanded something less technical and more human—a bright and optimistic brand that felt like the best the digital world has to offer. The name itself was inspired by the first line of "Auguries of Innocence," a poem by William Blake: "To see a world

 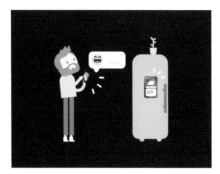 

Custom illustrations, animated for digital use

in a grain of sand." It connected to the Internet and the fiber-optic (glass) strands that deliver it to us, while also working well at different scales. Like many of the best names, it was at once intriguing and open to interpretation, but also simple and memorable.

Timescales meant we had to start on the identity design before the trademark registration was approved. We always aim for names that can be registered as "word-only" trademarks—they provide broader rights and protect the wording of the mark, regardless of its style, within your relevant classes.

We hire legal specialists when registering trademarks for our clients. Sure, we could save money by doing it ourselves, but why take the risk?

The presentation

We develop most of our work to an advanced stage before we present it. This includes an indication of how the identity works in application, which can be anything from a business card to a retail fascia, depending on where the brand will be most visible. For Grain, we showed them how it could work on van livery, as well as in advertising and on physical products such as routers.

We present one recommended solution with a maximum of two other routes because sharing many options is a form of insecurity. Unless each idea is equally as "right" as the others, it's an abdication of your responsibility as an expert. We always have a clear rationale why we believe our recommendation is the right solution, but any alternative routes must also meet our quality standards, and it's vital to never present anything you wouldn't be happy for the client to pick. The alternatives aren't variants on a theme—they're different ways of interpreting the strategy. The Grain project involved the presentation

of one alternative route, and the client agreed that our recommendation was the right one.

We always make it clear to clients that for the initial concepts stage we'll present one to three options. We'd challenge any brief that stipulated how many options the client wanted to see, and it's a red flag if a client wanted a guarantee that we'd keep producing options at no extra cost.

We encourage client critique on any aspect of our work, but it's our job, not theirs, to resolve issues.

After the presentation, we expect to refine and develop one of those options, addressing the client's feedback at the same time. We encourage client critique on any aspect of our work, but it's our job, not theirs, to resolve any issues. We always try to examine feedback in light of the strategy, getting the client to think in terms of right/wrong, as opposed to like/dislike (which is usually subjective). Potential clients who like to micromanage will quickly get the sense from us that we're not the people they're looking for.

Like every designer these days, we use mock-up templates to quickly convey our ideas. In most cases, we tend to edit them in such a way that they connect

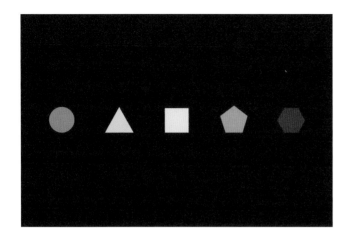

Let's get you connected.

GT WALSHEIM   CHARACTER

Light   abcdefghijklmnop
Regular   qrstuvwxyz
Medium   ABCDEFGHIJKLM
Bold   NOPQRSTUVWXYZ
                               0123456789
                               £€%@&#()<>.,:;*

Brand elements: shapes and type

to our visual aesthetic and tone. Often we will create our own, or work with other found imagery, to best communicate our visual ideas and language. We tend not to use presentation tools other than PDFs as we like the freedom and creative control of formatting with InDesign or Illustrator.

If it ever happened that the client didn't like the work we produced, we'd need to understand how we managed to get it wrong before considering how to respond. As every project stage is born from the one before, issues tend to arise earlier, which is what you want.

Developing guidelines

In the case of Grain, we scaled back the guidelines to meet the client's budget. We covered the essential elements in a simple PDF, with the intention to build on them over time. This approach makes sense because you can't properly define print specs, signage, paints, vinyls, digital experiences, and so on until you've tested them in application. Larger clients, for whom everything must be predetermined and implemented in advance of the launch, will naturally come with substantially larger project requirements on every level.

Guidelines combine two pieces—concrete aspects that are the fixed, fundamental rules, and fluid elements that show how the brand grows and evolves. On that basis, guidelines should be living documents. They should also reflect the brand as it currently is because the client will grow familiar with certain aspects of it long before the rest of the world does, so you need to exercise restraint over the fluid elements of the brand or it can end up losing focus.

Nothing is more dispiriting than seeing a great piece of work lose its way in the world. You're like a surrogate parent, creating something and then handing it over to people whom you hope will care for it as much as you do. Sometimes your work gets implemented in a way that you would have avoided. Our only defense against this happening is the strength of our relationship with our clients, and our ability to give advice that they recognize is in their best interests.

After completion

We try to ensure that any brand development project includes a retainer for ongoing support. It seems crazy that a client might spend significant sums of money on what will become a key strategic asset for the business and then not have any help protecting or managing that asset.

Key points

Communicating effectively with your client and keeping good records are two of the most important things you can do to avoid potential litigation.

Challenge any brief that stipulates how many options the client wants to see.

If client budgets are an issue, try looking for ways to limit the project scope or deliverables, and always make sure the client understands what's not included.

With naming projects, aim for names that can be registered as "word-only" trademarks—they provide broader rights and protect the wording, regardless of style.

When presenting identity options, you can present your client with one recommended solution coupled with a maximum of two other routes.

Sharing too many options is a form of insecurity, and unless each idea is equally as strong as the others, it's a neglect of your responsibility as the expert.

grainconnect.com

How

fast?

grainconnect.com

ARTISTS
ARTISANS
OLYMPIANS
VEGANS
BARISTAS
BREWERS
TECH HEADS
TATTOOISTS
BOOK BINDERS
VINTAGE FINDERS
SALMON SMOKERS
BUTTERFLY STROKERS
JEWELLERS
JOGGERS
BLOGGERS
BAKERS
MURAL MAKERS
DESIGNERS
DANCERS
SCULPTORS
WRITERS
ROOFTOP GARDENERS
PEDALLERS
PAINTERS
HAMMERS
CARPENTERS

Jack Renwick Studio

London
www.jackrenwickstudio.com

Project: Carpenters Wharf

*Carpenters Wharf is a property
consisting of thirty-five canal-side apartments
in London on Fish Island, Hackney Wick.*

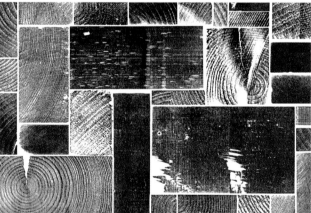

Letterpress prints of wood sourced from local businesses

We were introduced to the "4 Roach Road" project (as it was originally called), by a previous client who had enjoyed working with us and subsequently introduced us to their client.

Initial questions

Although there isn't a standardized set of questions we ask our clients, there's probably a lot of crossover. We always want our clients to tell us everything they possibly can about the project and what they're trying to achieve. When we understand their challenges, we can then work out what information is important and what else we need to know.

Carpenters Wharf was particularly interesting because we had two clients for this project—CBRE, the property manager, and Anderson, the property developer. As it was Anderson's first development in London, they also wanted to build their reputation, so it was equally important for us to discover their approach, values, and ambitions as a company, as well as those for the specific development.

Before receiving payment

The tasks we undertake before receiving the initial payment will often depend on the scope of the project and our relationship with the client. For this project, we carried out a recce, or reconnaissance, to experience the Fish Island neighborhood firsthand. It helped our understanding of what needed to be done, and we always learn much more about a project when seeing it in person with the client. We also prepared an initial creds deck—a document that explains our approach to work, how we think, and how that's relevant to their brief. Then we described our understanding of the project, clearly setting out the requirements and objectives, addressing "stupid"

or seemingly obvious questions early on, and making sure everyone is on the same page. That's important when starting a successful relationship.

When we visited Fish Island, we gained a sense of the local vibe and the target groups the apartments were aimed at, mostly professionals interested in immersing themselves in the vibrant surroundings. It made our kickoff presentation a lot more personal and illustrated our ambition to work with the client.

We always learn much more about a project when seeing it in person with the client.

Knowing what to charge

We base our fees primarily on how much time and how many people we will need to deliver the work. Each member has a set day rate to help our calculation. This approach allows us the flexibility to work on a range of quick, creative briefs, as well as yearlong behemoths.

We charge a fixed fee for most of our projects, based on our estimate of time and the type of work. We rarely charge by the hour unless it's for a time-based task—generally smaller parts of bigger jobs, such as artwork or content creation.

Architect's rendering of the development

When we started on Carpenters Wharf, we agreed to an initial fee that covered a base level of applications: the visual language, the brochure, website, print and billboard advertising, and the marketing suite. However, throughout the course of the project, we introduced other ideas for brand applications, marketing tools, and experiences. The client accepted these items, resulting in additional fees.

One of the extra ideas was to create permanent installations within the development. As the initial purpose of the brief was purely to sell apartments, it was fantastic to see the project become something more. The increased budget was also a great financial reward for us.

When you consider factors such as business rates and the increasing costs of doing business, it's only natural that our design fees have increased over the years. That said, one of our business models is to employ people who can add skills outside of the graphic design sphere. This has allowed us to offer our clients services such as illustration, copywriting, strategy, and animation design—services that we would normally outsource. As such, we've been able to charge more for our projects. As we gain more experience in what we do and the ability to deliver a better product, it's only right to raise our prices accordingly.

Price negotiation

A client should be able to negotiate fees, and we'd always prefer to discuss ways of making a project happen rather than simply missing out. We're often more willing to negotiate if the client works for a charity or a good cause, as there's typically more scope to be creative, as well as do some good!

There are times, however, when you just have to say no to a project. We take pride in our work, and we want to be able to do the best possible job for our clients. A trusting relationship can only be built when collaborating with a client that appreciates the value and impact of what we do and working with a reduced budget or time frame can compromise the outcome.

Estimating a project time frame

Determining how long a project will take comes down to experience and our knowledge about the client and type of job. There might also be the external factor of a specific client deadline. The deciding factor is ultimately the ambition of the brand. Rome wasn't built in a day, and a rushed rebrand is not going to take over a market sector.

There were many mini deadlines in the Carpenters Wharf project, as the client needed to begin marketing and promoting the site as early as possible, so a lot of time frames were driven by dates such as when the building work commenced. We initially outlined a time frame of approximately four months to deliver the visual language, brochure, website, print advertising, billboard work, and marketing suite. As the project developed, so did the client's ambition, and more was required of us. In the end, it took seven months to complete with the additional items.

Terms and conditions

We ask our clients to return a signed proposal before we start a job, just as we do with artwork approval.

We were once in the position where we needed to pursue legal help regarding payment. A client went

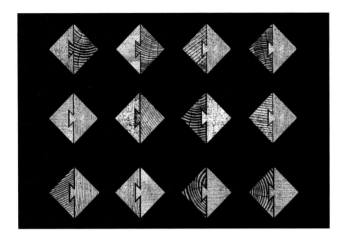

Development of dovetail joint symbol, logo, and signage

into liquidation after we'd worked on their project for more than a year, leaving us with several months of outstanding invoices. After getting legal advice, it became clear there wasn't much that could be done. It was a hard lesson learned.

Clients will occasionally push back on certain terms. More often than not, it's about simple things related to the way their businesses operate, which we can iron out, as we are generally flexible in the way we work. There are sometimes trickier questions regarding our ability to share the completed work or about intellectual property. This is why it's especially important to clarify expectations before beginning a project.

Handling payment

For larger projects, we generally divide payment to match the stages of the job, e.g., immersion and research, strategy, concepts, development, and implementation. We've found that this method helps us and the client. For smaller jobs, we take 50 percent in advance and 50 percent on completion or, if it's a client we've worked with many times, we'll occasionally take 100 percent on completion.

We generally receive payment by bank transfer, although we've sometimes received checks. We once took partial payment in shares for a start-up we were working with, but unfortunately the risk didn't pay off. Payment in shares can become complicated, but it's not something we'd instantly dismiss.

Many of our clients are based overseas, as far afield from the United Kingdom as Japan, but we always bill in British pounds sterling.

One of our clients, Wide Horizons, is an adventure learning charity. After creating their brand identity, we offered to design and install some environmental graphics at one of their centers. As payment, they gave us a weekend of kayaking, rappelling, and hiking in the Welsh valleys. It became our studio's summer party and brought a real feel-good factor to the end of a great project.

Conducting research

We do as much homework as we can before starting work, but we don't have any predefined method. It'll often depend on how we've been introduced to the client or what the process is going to be. We like to know about the client's market as soon as possible, both in terms of a visual and verbal audit, and how we can make a strategic difference to our client's business through design. It's never just a case of capturing information and playing it back—there needs to be insight into why certain details are important to the client and what that means for the job.

With Carpenters Wharf, we did a lot of research to understand Anderson, its London competitors, and the competitive context of property developments in the Hackney Wick area. What else is on sale there? Who's selling it? What are they saying? Why is our development different? It's important to avoid getting lost in market research; instead, look elsewhere for inspiration and discover how brands outside the sector behave and tell stories. This can help bring a fresh dimension to the project and create something that stands out in the market.

We deliberately didn't want to approach Carpenters Wharf like a property job, because the Hackney Wick area has a very creative, independent spirit. It became clear that Fish Island had an interesting history, too, and we worked with a London historian to find out more about the development and the local area. The knowledge gave us an authentic

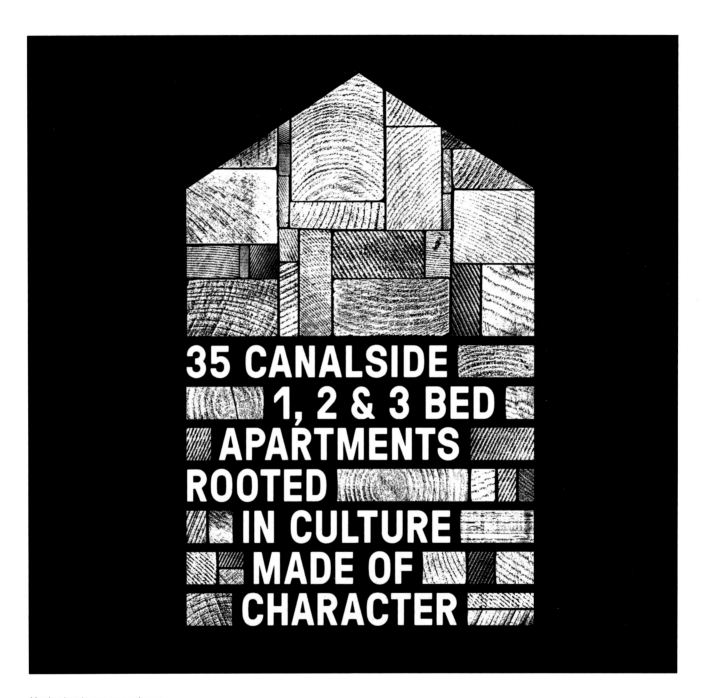

35 CANALSIDE
1, 2 & 3 BED
APARTMENTS
ROOTED
IN CULTURE
MADE OF
CHARACTER

Marketing imagery and copy

story to tell, and that became the basis for the naming and brand identity. Despite being a new development, we wanted to capture the romance of the past and embody that within the identity.

In a nutshell, research is about uncovering what the real issues are. A brief won't often include the real challenge. Doing our homework, walking in our clients' shoes, and looking at things with a fresh perspective puts us in a strong position to make great and valuable work together.

At the beginning of the Carpenters Wharf project, we spent a considerable amount of time experiencing life in the area, soaking up the atmosphere, drinking in the warehouse breweries, looking through the factory-converted galleries, and pouring over the graffiti-caked walls. There was a real sense of a town with its own identity, created by the local people and businesses.

Conducting thorough research gives us the opportunity to challenge the client and present them with a solution or insight they might've missed. These opportunities often occur, and it happened with Carpenters Wharf. Fish Island is renowned for its artists and graffiti, which is often beautiful, witty, and inspiring, but it is graffiti nonetheless. The developer and marketing agent had a preconceived idea that the identity should be based on graffiti and spray paint. Although that would've celebrated the area as it is today, would it celebrate the area that it will become? Would it provide any distinction or difference? Would it be authentic? We didn't want to present the development as a pastiche of East London street art. It had a much stronger and more authentic story to tell.

Because the client had expressed a desire to sell the apartments to people who already lived on Fish Island, we felt that rather than replicating the island

that everyone sees today, a far more compelling story would be to reveal a piece of the island's history that most people didn't know about.

Conducting thorough research gives us the opportunity to challenge the client and present them with a solution or insight they might've missed.

For fifty years, the development site was home to a luxury furniture maker that shipped timber down the canals. This, along with the physical appearance of the development, inspired the name Carpenters Wharf. Its history as a fine furniture factory felt in tune with the post-industrial nature of Fish Island. To bring the story to life without looking overly sentimental was one of our biggest challenges.

The direction we took sought to take the identity in a direction rooted in authenticity, and we devised a

Carpentry tools with embedded brand symbol

graphic system based on the wood stacks found in the timber yards that once populated the island. Working with a local letterpress artist, we used wood sourced from local businesses, artists, and craftspeople to create a bespoke set of prints. These prints were used throughout the marketing and communications materials, meaning that a genuine piece of Fish Island was included in every visual aspect of the brand.

The logo references the craft and expertise of the furniture makers through its dovetail joint, combining the letter C with the fish symbol. The typefaces used in the identity were chosen for their wood-based vernacular: GT Pressura is reflective of typography used to stamp wooden shipping crates, whereas GT Sectra resembles precise, wood-carved typography. In combination, the fonts further support the brand strategy of authenticity.

Setting the brief and defining the strategy

We always aim for agreement on a design brief, at least in principle, before beginning work on creative ideas. Briefs (as in the design task supplied to us) are becoming a rare occurrence. More commonly, we'll have a conversation with our clients, conduct research, and have a kick-off meeting with them to determine what the brief is. During the meeting, we revisit the idea of what a brand is. Two of the most important questions we usually ask are "Who is your audience and what do you want them to think about you?"

Carpenters Wharf was an entirely new brand with the sole purpose of selling the clients' apartments. It was commissioned to exist only until the apartments had been sold. For that reason, a lot of emphasis was put on who the target audience were, and how they could be reached.

Merging strategy and design

The high price point and low rental yield of properties in the development meant that Anderson and CBRE weren't targeting investors. Instead, they wanted sales from local, owner-occupiers—people who know and love Fish Island. The area is densely populated with artists, makers, and craftspeople, and many of the old factories and warehouses have been repurposed into thriving bars, breweries, restaurants, and workspaces. To effectively communicate to the right audience, our strategy was to visually celebrate the aesthetic of the building's striking architecture and reflect Fish Island's industrial history and vibrant creative character.

The visual identity of wood block prints and the key marketing message "Made of Character" became the foundation for a communication suite that looked authentic to the area, while still positioning the apartments at a premium price through the predominantly monochromatic color scheme.

When to stop experimenting

We're never satisfied, and we always want an extra day, hour, or minute. The most important thing is developing a strong idea and rationale—something you can present over the phone if needed. That way, if we haven't crafted the idea quite how we imagined, the concept still stands up to the test. We make sure that everyone in the studio has input and that ideas are up on the wall to review and discuss—whether you're working on the project or not. This helps us uncover the strongest solutions.

When in a creative rut

Press the ejector seat—get away from the desk and change your scenery. Go and look at something

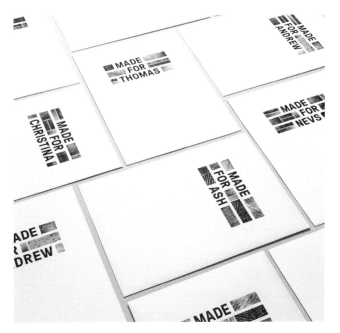

Sales collateral

completely unrelated. Avoid design blogs, Pinterest, and so on, and let chance play its part. Luckily, we're close to the Whitechapel Gallery and other wonderful sources of inspiration, but even a walk around the block can be enough to trigger a new thought.

Talking the project through among ourselves can also help, particularly when hearing from someone who isn't actively working on it. It's important not to spend longer than necessary on a task—someone or something will always help to bring a fresh perspective.

Presenting the work

The point at which our clients first learn of a specific design direction depends on the type and size of the job. There's often a strategic phase when we explore potential creative routes for the brand in question. It includes verbal and visual positioning, perhaps through mood boards and tone of voice—this can help to avoid any directions that don't resonate with the ambitions of the client. In projects without the strategic stage, we try to understand what the client is looking for through discussions and meetings and then move straight to the concept stage. Again, if you have a sound understanding, then a good idea should communicate itself. If the idea is strong, the visuals used to sell it can be fairly basic, and the polish is added during the development stage.

We create our presentations using InDesign, and we add context to our ideas through simple mock-ups we create in Photoshop, Illustrator, Marvel, and so on. We deliver the presentation in many different ways, but our first choice is to show slides using one of our laptops in person—there's no substitute for being in the room with the client, where you can read their reactions and control the speed of the presentation. However, many of our clients are overseas so we often must present via conference call. This has its technical (and time zone) difficulties but does work well. Occasionally we've flown to Japan to present using a translator; we had to steer clear of colloquialisms that could be translated in an entirely different way. We avoid emailing a PDF as much as possible, as that's not fair to the work or the client.

Two of the most important questions we usually ask are "Who is your audience and what do you want them to think about you?"

Number of ideas presented

Depending on the project time frame and budget, we generally present two to three ideas. We aren't scared of showing more, or less, if we feel it's right for the client. Three seems to be the magic number, though, because when presenting two options, if the client

All blocks end with a straight edge – flush to the edge of the type

Overlap type to help with readability

Space between blocks = roughly 1/15 size of cap/block height

1/15 X

X

REGISTER NOW

Tracking = 15
Leading = 0.9 x pt size

1/3 X

Space between blocks and type = 1/3 of cap/block height

Typography rules, promotional signage, and marketing suite installations

doesn't like one or feels that it's not relevant, the sense of not having a choice anymore can put them off the other option.

We agree at the beginning of the project how many ideas clients will see and include it in the proposal. It all goes back to building and maintaining a good relationship—the more comfortable the client feels with the process, the more confidence they have in you as an agency. That doesn't mean the number is always set in stone, and there have been times when we've had a last-minute thought and added a further, less developed option for discussion, but that only tends to pay off when you have built up enough trust with the client.

Reaching consensus

It's difficult to stay objective and avoid having a favorite design direction. If there is a clear favorite, then more often than not, the client will feel the passion when you present it—whether it's because we use more emotive language or pause slightly longer before moving on to the next concept. There are probably things we aren't even aware we're doing that can subtly sway a decision.

Clients often ask for our preferred route, even if they've already made up their mind. We're always happy to discuss our preference and why we think it will help to solve their challenges.

The only way to successfully guide the feedback you receive after a presentation is by having a strong rationale for the design choices you've made. The colors, the typefaces, and the photographic style must all be born from a core idea. You can't suggest a typeface just because it looks great and you want to use it—if you're challenged on it, you can't substantiate why you chose it.

When we're selecting the design elements, we'll often approach our rationale from the perspective of how the client would explain the design choices to their colleagues, family, and friends. The choices have to be clear enough for non-designers to understand and get behind.

To determine whether the options we present are strong enough, we always ask ourselves: Does this answer the brief? Is it relevant to the audience? Have we fulfilled what the proposal states? If, after the presentation, the client isn't happy, we try to find a compromise, which may include an additional budget.

Developing guidelines

There are two kinds of brand identity projects in this respect. Some identities require a rigid framework that works across every touchpoint without changing—e.g., use this typeface, this layout, put the logo here, and so on. Others need a few basic rules that leave a lot of room for a designer to express creative freedom and incorporate a directed way of thinking about the brand: What's the vision? What's our personality? What kind of lifestyle do our users embody? You see this more often in lifestyle or fashion brands where typefaces and colors can change at the drop of an Instagram post.

The majority of our clients ask us to create a set of guidelines. For Carpenters Wharf, however, no guidelines were needed because every touchpoint was created by our studio and the brand was essentially a marketing tool to sell the apartments.

A key strength of the Carpenters Wharf identity is in the relationship between the woodblocks and the typography. When we were able to find a workable relationship between the two, we created a brief set

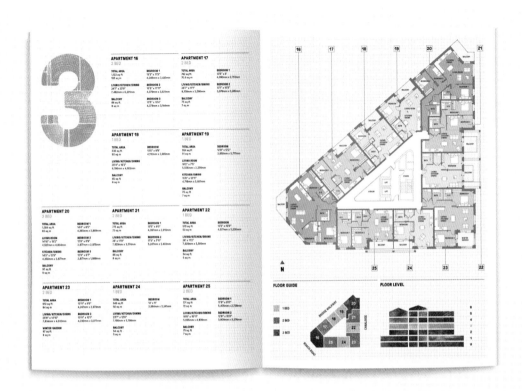

Sales brochure

of rules to ensure that all the brand applications were visually consistent.

We almost always supply guidelines as a PDF. There's often a considerable window of time when things are tweaked after the guidelines have been finished, and changes can include updating the photography with a new shoot that comes as a result of the rebrand. Creating digital, rather than print, guidelines helps in this regard and makes it easier to share the document throughout a company.

When working with a new brand, everyone in the organization should understand the choices we've made for the identity—what the logo means, why the typeface was selected, and what inspired the color scheme. If everyone who works with the brand believes in these choices, you have a much higher chance of ideas being implemented correctly.

Studio marketing

Most of our projects come from people we know, people we've previously worked for, or through recommendations from existing clients. Our motto is "Do good work for good people, then hope they tell someone else!"

We've seen an increase in inquiries because of our exposure on design blogs and in publications, and through winning a few awards, so it helps to be proactive about getting your work out there. We've even made contact with a few new clients through our Instagram feed, where we share a mix of new work, press, awards, and our studio culture. It's a great way of showing clients and other designers what we're about.

The Carpenters Wharf branding was well received in the design press, and successful in design awards.

That brought a lot more inquiries from potential clients, as well as a huge increase in our social media following. We haven't tried buying advertising, whether print or online. Building and maintaining relationships is about as strategic as we've gotten with our marketing.

Key points

You can base your charges primarily upon how much time you feel is needed to deliver the work and how many people are required for the task.

For larger projects, one option is to divide payment by job stages, e.g., immersion and research, strategy, concepts, development, and implementation. For smaller jobs, it's more common to seek 50 percent in advance and 50 percent on completion.

The more comfortable the client feels with the process, the more confidence they'll have in you as an agency.

Presenting three ideas can be beneficial because when you present two and the client doesn't like one of them, they then lose the sense of having a choice, which can put them off the other.

When selecting individual design elements, consider approaching your rationale from the perspective of what the client would tell their colleagues. The choices have to be clear enough for non-designers to understand.

If everyone in an organization who works with the identity believes in your design choices, you have a much higher chance of people correctly implementing your ideas.

KING'S CROS

BOND
STREET

OLD ST

SHO

SOHO

CITY OF

ST

MAYFAIR

WESTMINSTER

LONDON

SOUTHBANK

LON

BRI

WATERLOO

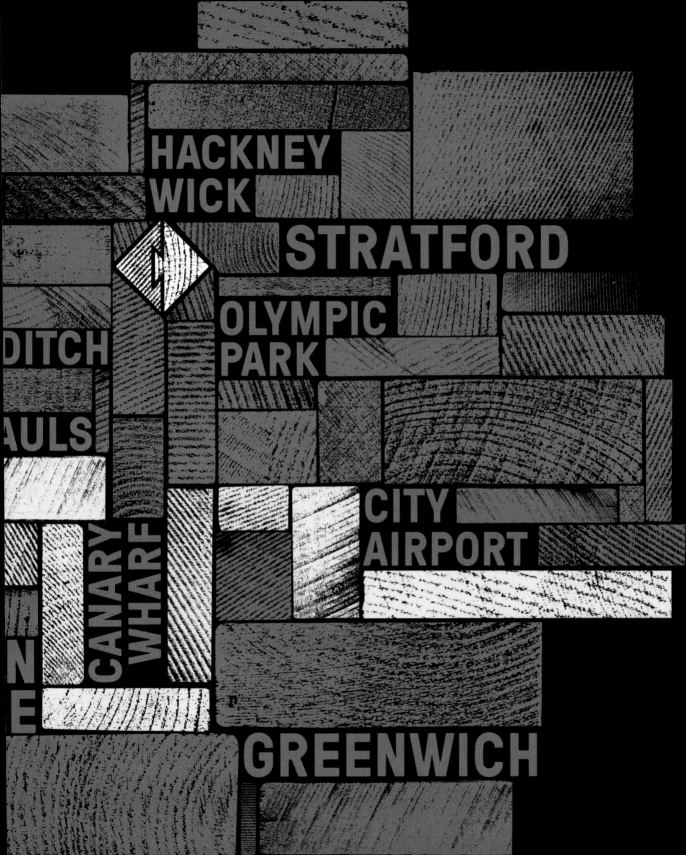

burstoralcare.com

burstoralcare.

TOP-UP PACK
1x BURST replacement head
1x toothpaste

TOP-UP PACK
1x BURST replacement head
1x toothpaste

ico Design

London
www.icodesign.com

Project: Burst

*Burst is an oral care brand with
a bold ambition—to position itself
as a challenger to revolutionize the staid,
overpriced oral care industry.*

Two of the unused concepts (top and bottom)
explored during the experimentation stage

Our introduction to the client came through a mutual contact who was an early investor. He felt that the client needed a strong brand partner to guide him through to launch, as he'd developed a great product but would need help building a brand that fit his ambition.

Initial questions

Our first meeting was rather tense. The client had employed a freelance designer to produce some concepts and we expressed our thought that they didn't capture the attitude and opportunity that was apparent for the project. We'd also canvassed the opinion of a contact who'd worked in innovation at a large beauty retailer, and her thoughts backed up ours. A week or so after the meeting, when the client had time to consider our feedback, he returned to our studio and appointed us brand partners.

No two client conversations are the same.

No two client conversations are the same, but one thing we always try to determine is their dedication to the project and receptiveness to creativity. We work with many start-ups and speak to a lot of people with great ideas and products, and the attribute we look for above all others is ambition—we want to work with people determined to build brands that can grow. This client perfectly fit this profile—he'd previously had success with another toothbrush and had designed the high-quality Burst brush. He had

a proven track record and was so committed that he moved to Los Angeles shortly after our first meeting to launch Burst in the United States.

Project deliverables

Like many branding projects, defining an exact list of deliverables at the beginning was never going to be possible. In fact, both we and the client had only a broad notion of the project's scope. We knew Burst would need packaging for the toothbrush and replacement heads, an e-commerce website, and custom photography, but how the project would grow beyond these applications was difficult to gauge. In the early stage of such a project, however, it's critical to prioritize key applications.

We could give an estimate for the initial brand identity creation, but we had to approach other aspects as separate projects. With the packaging, for example, we worked on developing several custom packaging solutions, followed by many iterations before the final approval.

Tasks before payment

Burst needed to raise significant capital to create an e-commerce website and fulfill its first orders. We've long recognized the value that investors place on a brand—speaking to potential investors with a fully-rounded concept makes your company far more attractive. This creates an issue for a branding agency, however, because it means defining a brand strategy and creating a brand identity before the client has the funds to pay for it.

After discussions with the client, we agreed to rapidly develop the brand, fast-tracking art direction, photography, tone of voice, packaging design, and so on, so that Burst would be fully realized before

Behind the scenes at the photoshoot

investment. We did a lot of work up front (even helping with a pitch presentation for potential investors) with the agreement that as soon as funds had been raised, we'd be paid a lump sum to offset the completed tasks. In the short term, we received a modest monthly retainer, taking a gamble that we'd be paid fully after successful fund-raising.

The trust and belief we showed in both the client and the product have led to a strong relationship and has allowed us to convert some outstanding fees into equity in the rapidly growing company. The equity-for-fees model is an approach we've taken for a number of projects, but it's by no means perfect for every client. In fact, we'd only suggest it in special cases—essentially when a brand wants to grow quickly and create significant monetary value. It's no good owning shares in a company when there's little possibility of cashing out.

Determining what to charge

We're probably similar to most studios in that we base our fees on the time we think a project will take. With Burst, we were able to put a fee on creating the brand identity, but then a large number of projects followed on an ad-hoc basis—many of which would have been incredibly time consuming to quote for.

Instead of agreeing on a fee that might cover every individual element, we negotiated an ongoing retainer based on an average number of hours we'd work per month. We share our hours with the client, and the retainer fee increases accordingly if we exceed those hours. A relationship like this will only work when there's mutual trust.

Like any agency, we price higher for the creation of a "true" branding project (such as Burst)—one that demands an immersion phase, strategic direction,

naming, and so on, rather than a simple visual identity creation, such as for a stand-alone restaurant.

For larger proposals, assigning fees to project stages gives us leverage should the project demand more work than initially anticipated—perhaps because the client shifts the brief slightly, they can't reach a consensus on the creative work, or their chosen brand name might fall through after further research.

For larger proposals, assigning fees to project stages gives us leverage should the project demand more work than initially anticipated.

Over the years, our rates have grown in line with inflation and also because the agency has grown and our overhead expenses have increased, but we're still reasonably priced for a mid-size agency.

Photos overlaid on the brand patterns

There are only a few cases when we might be open to negotiating our fee. These include a new client who offers a long-term commitment; an existing client who wants a small job as a favor; and occasionally a project we accept for well-considered business reasons, e.g., to open up work in a new sector.

Estimating the project duration

For a brand creation project, we can give pretty accurate time lines for the immersion and brand strategy, creation, and refinement phases. This might typically last about eight weeks, depending on the client sign-off process. Estimating the time for content creation and artwork rollout is more difficult because they demand shooting films, conceiving of a photoshoot, or even waiting for a client to find a retail space.

Burst was different to many of our branding projects because we knew we were in it for the long run and that there'd be a lot of work.

Invoicing and receiving payment

How we divide our project fees depends on the client and size of the project. In general, we invoice small jobs of £10,000 ($13,000) or less on completion. For larger brand projects, we invoice at key project milestones and deliverables—25 percent each on commission, brand strategy presentation, creative concept presentation, and final brand completion and delivery. We ensure that the rates reflect the work we've undertaken, the client understands the value involved, and we're fairly paid for what we do.

We use Deltek's TrafficLIVE software to run time sheets and prepare project quotes and invoices. We don't send receipts back to clients, but we provide clearly detailed account summaries, depending on the size of project.

Clients generally pay by bank transfer, but we try to be flexible when they suggest alternative payment methods. The payment process isn't different for overseas clients, but we might ask for a larger amount up front. If projects are quoted in foreign currency, we use the exchange rate at the time of quotation, and our contracts state that any fluctuations in exchange rates will be reflected in the billable fees, subject to the degree of fluctuation and the total value of the project.

Research and strategy

The first stage of any project is immersion, when we get to know the client, their motivations, and insights. We conduct workshops and interviews with key client stakeholders, read any research they've carried out, become familiar with key competitors, and visit any sites if the project involves a retail element. We research consumer motivations and create personas. We also do our own research to uncover strategic and creative insights rather than fundamentally define a client's business.

When we receive a particularly vague project brief, we draft our own brief for the client to sign off on before we begin work. Essentially, we'll write the brief if the client can't. For example, an initial client brief might say, "We want a brand for our new iced tea." Before we do any creative work, we immerse ourselves enough to agree on a more fitting brief. A change may be as straightforward as "Design a visual identity for an iced tea brand with a South African theme to appeal to sporty millennials and for launch in American and British markets."

We give as detailed a brief as possible in our proposal, broken into stages: immersion; brand strategy, creation, and refinement; content and artwork creation; and rollout.

From the brand gallery

Smart, strategic thinking underpins every robust brand—that means it understands its audience, defines an ownable position in the market, identifies the creative opportunity, and describes its behavior, personality, and mission. The development of the visual identity comes as a response to the strategic platform.

We don't have a specific house style for translating strategy into design visuals, and we constantly look for the most creative, appropriate solution. This is where experience and cultural awareness count—knowing which solution is correct, and why. Sometimes that might be driven by the tone of voice of the brand, other times it's an approach to art direction. Graphic design on its own is only part of the solution. With Burst, for example, the disruptive energy of the brand came through in the photography and dynamically colored patterns—it isn't explicit in the logo. In other projects, the logo might express more personality, or a distinctive tone of voice can play a large part.

Ideas and experimentation

We have constant reviews throughout our design development work. One of our partners and our creative director will guide the process, eliminating ideas that don't work and focusing on the ones that do. The design process is like a funnel: there are numerous ideas at the start that get narrowed down to one or two crafted, robust ideas at the end.

If we feel it's appropriate, we'll meet with the wider team to brainstorm ideas and dismiss the more obvious ones that might be clichés in disguise. Like any creative endeavor, brainstorming needs focus—it shouldn't just be a free-for-all.

Copyright and trademarking

We always insist that a client works with an attorney when trademarking a name or identity, and we stress that this task is outside the scope of our work.

The development of the visual identity comes as a response to the strategic platform.

We do due diligence with our creative work to help avoid infringement, and we completely familiarize ourselves with our client's competitive environment. Due to the sheer number of logos in the world (now readily available on the Internet), it's impossible to create one that's entirely unique. Occasionally, halfway through a project, we've found similarities between our work and something that already exists, making us shift direction.

It's slightly irritating when we release work and an ill-informed person points out that our logo for a legal firm in London is "obviously a rip-off of this small hotel logo in Denver." We can't stress enough that no credible studio ever willingly copies logos—yet we can all point out identities that look like others. Give any designer the Internet and they could find similar logos for most studios' outputs.

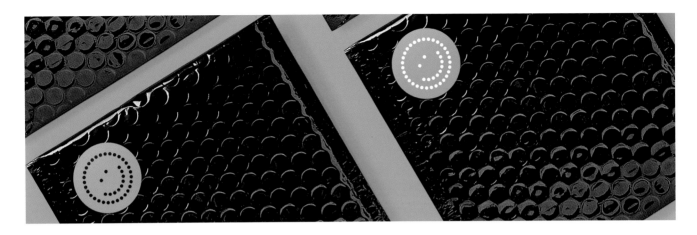

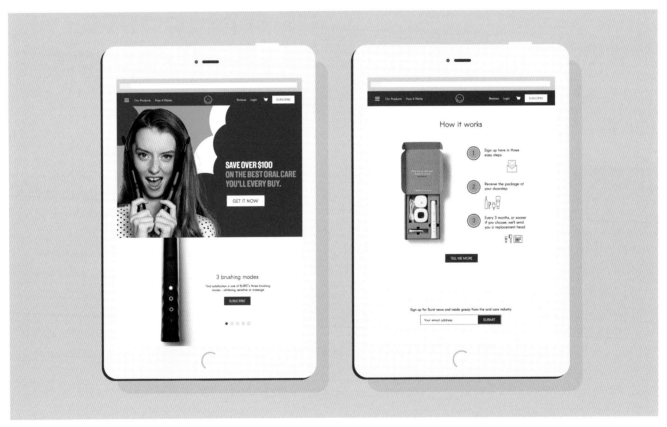

Packaging and web design

On the other hand, there are blatant rip-offs out there, too. One of our brands, Snog frozen yogurt, has been copied time and time again, often by companies in the food and beverage industries. When we see our work being copied, we simply let the designer responsible know we've seen it. Hopefully that's shame enough to put a stop to it.

We typically show two creative routes for brand identity projects and often one if we feel completely confident in the approach.

The presentation

At the start of the creative process, we often share a series of mood boards with the client to quickly test a design direction or approach. This is particularly useful if a client struggles with articulating their thoughts. For instance, if we're creating an identity for a beauty brand and a client wants a "mix of science and nature," we'll present mood boards

that show various scales of science versus nature to gauge exactly which balance the client likes the most. This approach works well for projects with smaller budgets because it shortcuts the process of creating fully-realized design directions.

We deliver the majority of our presentations on screen and Keynote is our go-to presentation tool. We develop the design work almost exclusively using Adobe Creative Suite. We find Pixeden useful for producing mock-ups, but we're building a collection of our own blank templates because Pixeden visuals are becoming increasingly clichéd. We also use InVision to show digital projects, and we have an in-house filmmaker enabling us to present an entire concept as a film—we did this when we presented our identity for London Luton Airport to shareholders.

We typically show two creative routes for brand identity projects and often one if we feel completely confident in the approach. Although there are agencies that present five or six routes, we think this shows a lack of leadership and expertise because part of an agency's role is to provide good advice and act as editors as well as advisors. With three or more routes, you are essentially providing too much arbitrary choice and not enough guidance. We self-edit creative routes in-house during the process and then show the client a visual scrapbook of our work, explaining why we chose not to fully develop various options. By doing so, we only present creative directions that we have absolute faith in and we eliminate any chance of a client choosing what would be our third or fourth preference.

Clients will always know in advance how many ideas we'll present. We clearly define what they'll expect, and we never overpromise.

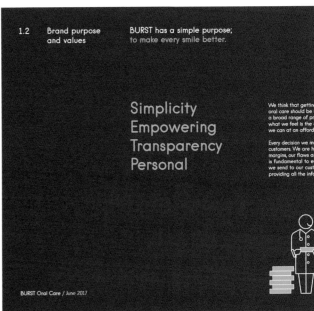

BURST has a simple purpose; to make every smile better.

Simplicity
Empowering
Transparency
Personal

We think that getting
oral care should be s
a broad range of pro
what we feel is the c
we can at an affordo

Every decision we ma
customers. We are ho
margins, our flaws an
is fundamental to eve
we send to our custo
providing all the info

BURST Oral Care / June 2017

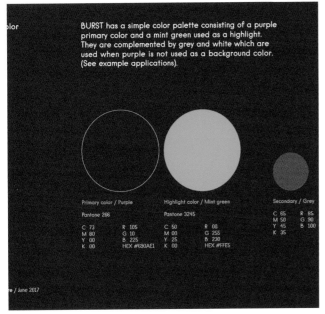

...olor

BURST has a simple color palette consisting of a purple primary color and a mint green used as a highlight. They are complemented by grey and white which are used when purple is not used as a background color. (See example applications).

Primary color / Purple

Pantone 266

C 73   R 105
M 80   G 10
Y 00   B 225
K 00   HEX #690AE1

Highlight color / Mint green

Pantone 3245

C 50   R 00
M 00   G 255
Y 25   B 230
K 00   HEX #FFE5

Secondary / Grey

C 65   R 85
M 50   G 90
Y 45   B 100
K 35

...re / June 2017

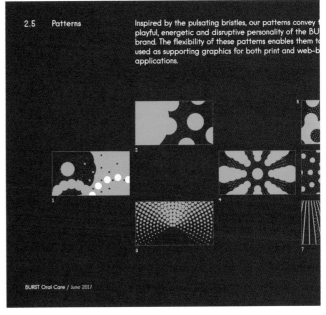

Inspired by the pulsating bristles, our patterns convey t playful, energetic and disruptive personality of the BU brand. The flexibility of these patterns enables them to used as supporting graphics for both print and web-b applications.

BURST Oral Care / June 2017

A small sample from the brand guidelines

Reaching consensus

At the end of a presentation, a client will normally ask us for our preferred direction. The important thing is for our entire agency to agree on our preference beforehand because we have to act as a trusted advisor.

We stress the importance of a visual identity responding to the agreed-on strategy and impress on the client that the work we create is for their core audience, not our collective personal tastes. A little pushback is common, however, and our response is a matter of being confident in our choices and knowing when we're not going to win an argument.

Occasionally a client won't like what we present, and we'll demand particularly focused feedback before we do any further work. There was an occasion when we presented four strong identity concepts for a brand, the last two in response to the client's initial feedback when they didn't like our first presentation. After the second round, it was clear to us that the client was never going to make a decision, so we parted ways. It's been a couple of years and they still haven't addressed their branding.

Developing guidelines

Guidelines are a separate cost for the client, and we usually present them in a short PDF. In truth, many smaller projects don't require a comprehensive document, but for those that do, we always recommend they be produced after the assets are created. Guidelines without real applications are bit of a misnomer.

Increasingly, brands have shorter lifespans, and the process of iteration often begins as soon as they're launched. As such, a massive set of printed guidelines is practically a thing of the past, though digital guidelines are still useful for bringing coherence and clarity to a new brand and steering it through a rapid growth phase.

Key points

With many branding projects, defining a comprehensive list of deliverables at the beginning is impossible.

Fees are based on the estimated time frame for project completion.

The equity-for-fees model is an approach you should only consider if the brand wants to create significant monetary value in a short time frame.

The proposal is broken into stages: immersion; brand strategy, creation, and refinement; content and artwork creation; and rollout.

If trademarking a name or identity is outside your skill set, insist that your client works with a trademark lawyer.

Although we can all point out identities that look like others, no credible design firm will ever willingly copy a logo.

When more than one designer is involved in presenting more than one option to a client, it's important that all designers agree on the preferred direction beforehand.

The client should understand that the work you create is for their core audience, not the collective personal tastes of the client and the designer.

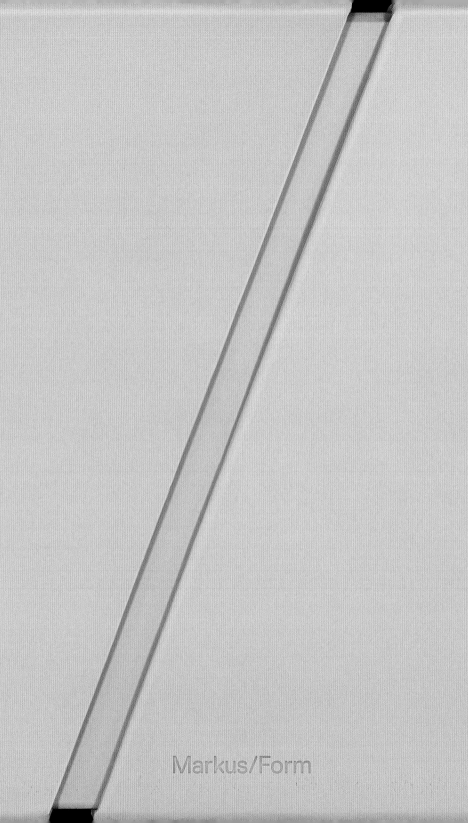

Markus/Form

Lundgren+Lindqvist

Gothenburg
www.lundgrenlindqvist.se

Project: Markus Form

Markus Form is a Swedish furniture company founded by architect Markus Nydén. Markus's idea is to revitalize the Swedish furniture industry, with the ambition to develop and produce relevant furniture that's practical, easy to match, and environmentally friendly.

Product photography

The client first approached us in early 2014, after they had commissioned a Stockholm-based studio in Sweden to design their visual identity. The design studio's proposal lacked insight into the furniture business and bore a striking resemblance to the visual identity of an already established, international furniture company, according to the client. As a consequence, Markus Form chose to end the relationship with the studio, and contacted us. With the disappointment from their previous attempt fresh in mind, the founder initially wanted to meet with us for a more philosophically-oriented talk, rather than a typical briefing session.

During our first meeting, we spent several hours discussing everything from politics to the state of the Swedish furniture industry, hardly ever touching on standard topics such as project requirements, budgeting, and the project's time frame. It turned out that, although we had chosen different disciplines, we shared a passionate interest in both design and architecture, and were very much aligned in our aesthetic preferences.

Similar meetings followed, filled with heated yet friendly discussions and exchanges of anecdotes. Having spent many years in the business, Nydén had amassed a collection of stories on everyone from the Finnish modernist Alvar Aalto to the Swedish master architect Sigurd Lewerentz. We formed a strong relationship, along with a sense of mutual respect and trust.

After the previous, failed attempt at designing the new visual identity, our client's founder spent extensive time researching design studios around the world and making a list of requirements for the project. The fact that we both are based in Sweden was more of a chance occurrence than something that influenced Markus Form's choice in making us their design studio.

Initial questions

We are always interested in a company's raison d'être. We prefer to work with clients who have a clear vision and aim to be the best at what they do. With Markus Form, we wanted to hear their thoughts on topics such as why the world needs more chairs when there are already thousands of options available. Questions about sustainability led to further discussions. The client argued that using the most environmentally-friendly materials doesn't always lead to the most sustainable product, and that a product's ability to withstand wear and tear is often overlooked, or a low priority, in our time of fast consumption and trend-led decision-making.

The questions we ask a client differ somewhat depending on whether they are a young or well-established company. Our oldest client was founded in 1681 and, during their centuries in business, they have chiseled out a clear strategy. Whereas when we first met Markus Form, the company didn't even have a name.

Project deliverables

Even though our client had already formed the skeleton of a basic strategic structure for the project, the scope grew exponentially from the time of our first meeting, and many deliverables were added during the course of the five years that we've worked together. The initial project encompassed naming;

Markus Form: Buddy

Buddy is a small, useful piece of furniture that could be placed anywhere within a space and in many different environments. Buddy is available in two sizes and in a limited range of colours. The solid wood base contrasts with the cold metal surface of the aluminium bowl, adding a warm filigree character to the object and creates an iconic and graceful appearance.

M/BUDDY	⊞ MADE IN SWEDEN	SMALL	LARGE
TRIPOD	ASH WOOD, LACQUER	590 MM (HEIGHT)	820 MM (HEIGHT)
BOWL	ALUMINIUM, COATED	BOWL	385 MM (DIAMETER)

"I think a remarkable accomplishment in today's design world is emotion as an additional value. Especially in comparison with design of the early 20th century, where objects were created mainly to satisfy needs of people induced by external circumstances, we are today allowed to design not only functionally but also emotionally."

Bao-Nghi Droste – Designer of Buddy

FEEDBACK. WE WOULD APPRECIATE TO GET YOUR FEEDBACK AND TO SEE BUDDY IN YOUR HOME OR OFFICE. PLEASE EMAIL COMMENTS AND PHOTOS TO BUDDY@MARKUSFORM.SE

Markus/Form

Functional Furniture for Modern Day Needs

Markus Form is a Swedish furniture company founded with the idea of revitalising Swedish furniture design and an ambition to develop and produce relevant furniture, that is practical, easy to match and kind on the environment.

Inspiration and knowledge comes from the heritage of Swedish and Scandinavian furniture and design, where the form is often strongly influenced by ergonomics and functionality as well skilled artisanship and a good working knowledge of materials.

Our collection will be developed to contain strong individualistic pieces with clear shared qualities in both common furniture typologies and new ones. Characterised by excellent function, answering to everyday needs, our furniture will be functional and adaptable for a long time to come.

Please visit markusform.se for more information on our company and our growing range of products.

MARKUS FORM AB, BOX 4426, 203 15 MALMÖ, SWEDEN. ONLINE: MARKUSFORM.SE
EMAIL ADDRESS: INFO@MARKUSFORM.SE · TELEPHONE NUMBER: 0046 702 767 609

Swing-tags and photography

the design of their visual identity; a full range of stationery, including a rich system of contracts and order forms; strategic consulting in the shaping of their business plan; and the design and development of their website.

As the client finalized their first products, the project grew to include packaging, such as hangtags and envelopes for loose components and stamps and labels for the exterior of the wrapping.

Working closely with the company's founder, and photographer Kalle Sanner, we also meticulously crafted a brand story based around photographic essays, where the universal appeal of the products is always the starting point. To date, we have shot Markus Form's products in at least twenty different locations, ranging from a haunted bed-and-breakfast to a bronze foundry.

Our policy requires an up-front payment of 50 percent of the project's total cost.

Before receiving payment

We require an initial payment of 50 percent of the project's total cost up front. Payment tends to vary,

as larger projects such as this one are often split into different phases, which we invoice separately.

We start the project when we receive this initial deposit. Up until that point, we are only prepared to meet to establish whether we and the client are right for each other and to scope out the project, enabling us to provide the client with a cost and time estimate. Of course, with established clients, this policy is not as important as it is with new clients.

Working terms

We usually follow a structure that includes an initial briefing, followed by a debriefing. For us, the most successful projects are built around a sense of strong, mutual trust. We emphasize this during our initial client meetings, where we also stress that it's not just them choosing to work with us, but also us choosing to work with them. The privilege of being a small studio is that we have the opportunity of turning down projects that we may feel, for different reasons, are not for us.

For new digital projects, we have terms stating that the work we do is limited for use on a single domain or in a certain context, and that a website cannot be resold as a theme or cloned to set up new businesses. Sometimes modularity and the opportunity to multiply a site is a requirement on behalf of the client, and in those cases, an additional licensing fee may apply.

In cost estimates, we leave certain tasks or deliverables as optional or open. An example of this is the time required for corrections, which is usually very difficult to estimate at the beginning of a project.

Clients querying the terms

A frequent topic of discussion is intellectual

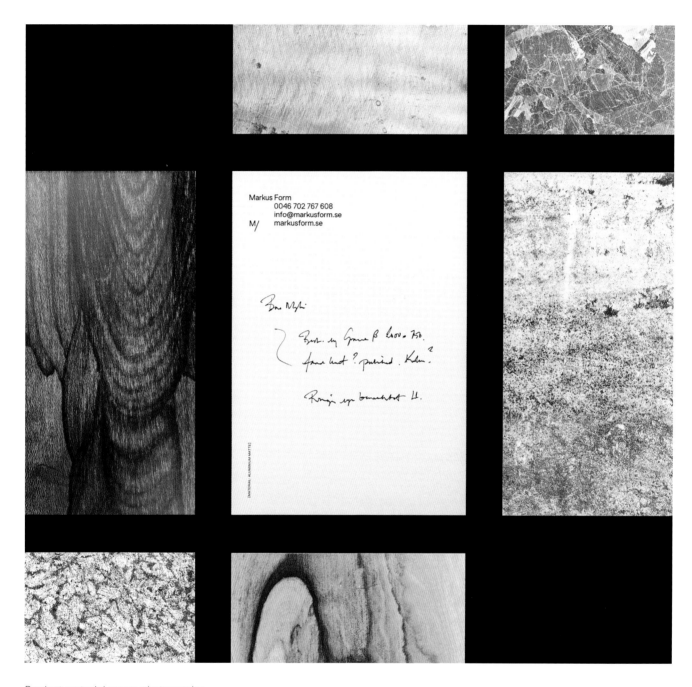

Markus Form
0046 702 767 608
info@markusform.se
M/   markusform.se

[MATERIAL: ALUMINIUM MATTE]

Product material macro photography,
used on the back of correspondence cards

property, i.e., if and how clients are allowed to alter our work for future use. In some projects, say a stationery range for a growing company, we deliver open, editable documents, while in others, we may take care of everything from the actual design to handling the contact with the printer and other production partners.

In many cases, such as in the case of a logotype we've designed, the client will, of course, own the rights to the work we do for them. However, that doesn't automatically mean that they can alter the work in any way they see fit.

We also have varying minimum levels of time required to deliver work that lives up to the high level of quality we see as an absolute requirement. If it was necessary to compromise on this, the quality of our work would be affected, so we'd prefer to turn the project down.

When it comes to our clients agreeing to our terms, a signed contract is our usual form of agreement, but sometimes confirmation through email or over the phone will do—it depends on the size of the project and our relationship with the client.

When things didn't go to plan

One situation that kept us on our toes and made us realize just how important a contract and deposit payment are, was a project we worked on from 2013 to 2014.

The client was a start-up in Switzerland, working within the wider field of architecture and construction. The company was headed by a very elegant and affluent man, with two degrees and an impressive curriculum vitae. The company wanted us to design a visual identity and packaging system.

The first meeting was conducted via Skype, with the client located in his office in a villa designed by one of the master architects of the modernist era.

The project and client both seemed promising, and we left the meeting with a feeling of excitement. The client was in a hurry and wanted us to get started as quickly as possible, which meant that there was little time to wait for a down payment—the client promised they would sort it out as soon as the founder had returned from a business trip abroad. Based on our excitement, and the impression projected by the founder, we sidestepped our usual administrative routine and started immediately. We rescheduled a few other commitments and worked long hours and weekends.

After two weeks, we still hadn't received the initial payment, so we called the client, who was seemingly surprised and apologetic, and said they would call their bank and ask them why there had been a delay. A few days later, the founder, who was again very apologetic, contacted us to say that his assistant had mistakenly transferred the money to the wrong account and that they were now working to get it all sorted out. We could expect to receive the payment shortly.

We continued working on the project for another week and completed a large part of the project's initial scope. As there was still no sign of the initial payment, we contacted the client and said that we'd have to pause the project until it was received.

At this point, the client made themselves completely unavailable to us, refusing to answer the phone or respond to our emails. With a substantial amount of money owed to us for the work we had done, the client disappeared and was never heard from again.

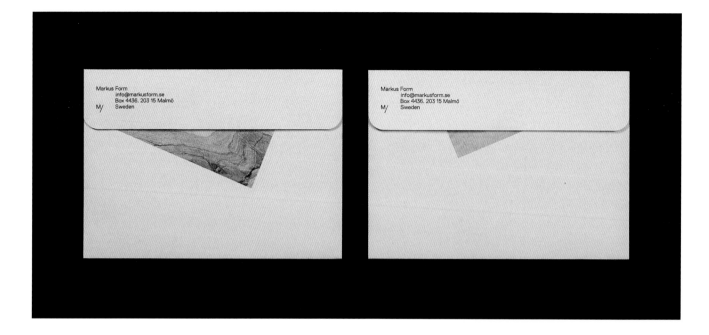

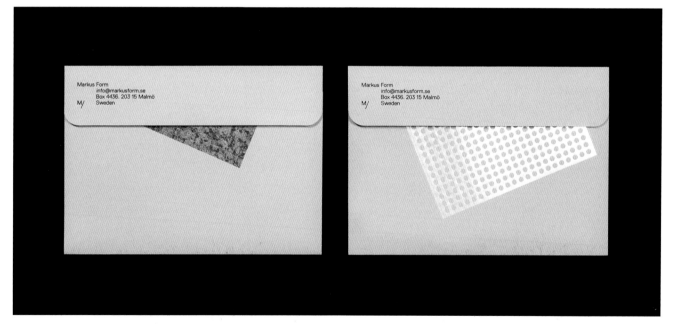

Envelopes

Two years later, a case study for the same project and client, designed by another design studio, appeared in a renowned international design magazine. We contacted the studio, with whom we were loosely acquainted, and told them about our experience with the client. As it turned out, they had a very similar experience, and only decided to show the project to get something out of the situation.

The lesson we learned is that appearances can be deceiving. Making a few requirements of your client before getting started on a new project will take you a long way.

Making a few requirements of your client before starting a new project will take you a long way.

For projects that we could potentially have needed to consult lawyers, we decided that it would likely cost us more, in terms of time, money, and energy, than it would to just let the situation go. It's important to be able to hold your ground and not let clients treat you as a pushover yet, at the end of the day, being a small studio, we can spend our time more wisely than getting involved in lengthy legal battles.

Determining what to charge

The size of the client often affects the time we have to spend on a project. With a larger client, the number of stakeholders grows, thereby increasing the complexity.

Our fees are always determined by the estimated time we'll have to spend on a project. Often this is also partially influenced by budget restrictions on behalf of the client.

While we've worked on and off with Markus Form for the last five years, the initial project was completed over a three-month period, during which we also worked on projects for other clients.

Usually our pricing for a visual identity project starts around 91,000 in Swedish krona ($10,000), going upward depending on the scope. That being said, we also work for independent artists and charitable organizations and, in those instances, our pricing will look very different.

There is almost always a fee negotiation. Most of the time, it comes down to what the client can spend and how much time the project requires. The usual outcome is that that we find a middle ground that allows us to spend a sufficient amount of time on the project while the client stays within their defined budget.

Clients rarely question our fees, but it does happen. Being a small studio, we apply a flat rate hourly fee, so there's no difference between an hour spent by a designer or a developer. Although we might not all be involved in the projects we accept, our most senior staff oversee everything that leaves the studio.

Offering pricing options

Many of our proposals include various options, allowing us to tailor the project and balance the client's needs with their budget. For a website, a

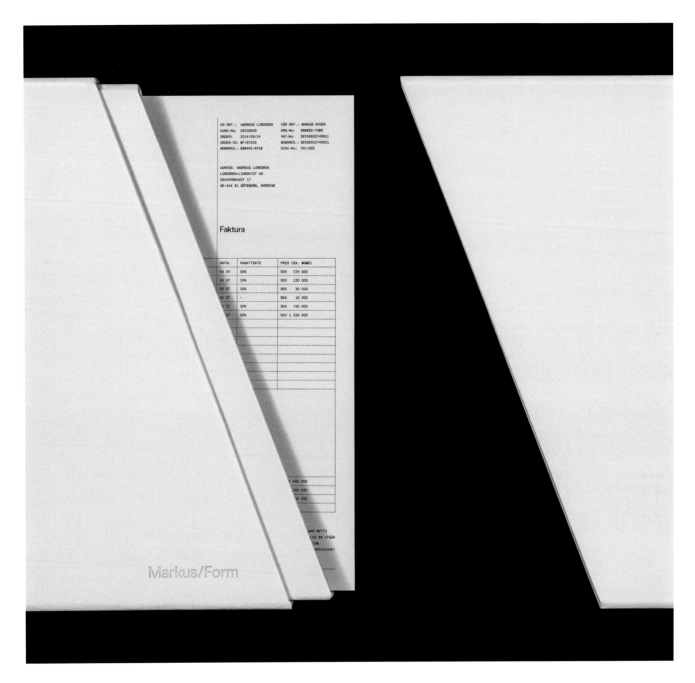

ER REF.: ANDREAS LUNDGREN   VÅR REF.: MARKUS NYDÉN
KUND-No: 00225809   ORG-No: 656933-7495
ORDER: 2014/09/24   VAT-No: SE556933749501
ORDER-ID: WF/BT023   MOMSREG.: SE556933749501
MOMSREG.: 556441-6715   SIDA-No: 001/002

ADRESS: ANDREAS LUNDGREN
LUNDGREN+LINDQVIST AB
SOCKERBRUKET 17
SE-414 51 GÖTEBORG, SVERIGE

Faktura

ANTAL	RABATTSATS	PRIS (EX. MOMS)
40 ST	30%	SEK 224 000
24 ST	20%	SEK 120 000
06 ST	10%	SEK 30 000
01 ST	-	SEK 10 000
ST	30%	SEK 720 000
ST	20%	SEK 1 336 000

1 440 000
360 000
00 000

GÅR NETTO
LUS 8% UTGÅR
TUM.
KYLDIGHET

Markus/Form

Document holder

second pricing option may include the design and development of an online store that might not have been in the original scope, allowing us to show the client opportunities for expanding their business and increasing their revenue.

Some clients have a very clear idea of what they need, while others turn to us for input. By including optional items in the proposal, we also enable the client to plan their future budget more accurately should they wish to add something to the project at a later stage.

Invoicing and payment

A typical project for us includes the design of a visual identity and the design and development of a website. We divide these projects into two main phases, one encompassing the visual identity and potential physical items, and the other the website. These two main phases will likely have subphases, such as the design of the website being one, and the website development being another. We invoice each of the main phases separately. When building larger websites, we may divide the invoicing into four payments to avoid long periods without any money coming in.

The most usual method of payment is by bank transfer. Many of our American clients prefer to pay by check, which we try to avoid, as Swedish banks have become rather restrictive in accepting checks and apply high fees to these transactions. We also try to avoid PayPal payments because these mean additional work for our bookkeepers.

For international clients, prices are specified in euros, while proposals for local clients are specified in Swedish krona. When converting our hourly rate to euros, we add a slight margin in the conversion to protect ourselves from currency dips.

Pricing advice

Know the value you can bring to a project, but also be conscious of how valuable the right project can be in relation to bringing in other projects with larger budgets. This is not to say that you should work for free, but it is usually better to work for little money than not to work at all.

In our early years in business, we spent parts of the very limited budgets we were given on increasing the quality of print production for the client's stationery, despite it often meaning there would be little revenue left for us.

Conducting research

For this project, the client's area of business happened to be very close to our own personal interests, which meant we didn't have to start from scratch. We also had extensive experience working with clients in the field of architecture, which helped a great deal. In addition, the company's knowledgeable founder proved to be a great resource, and the bulk of the research was conducted over several meetings and discussions with him. Of course, we also looked carefully at the competition and the company's primary demographics, ranging from architects and interior designers to design-savvy homeowners.

During the initial phase of a project, our main task is to ask the right questions and listen carefully to the client and, in some cases, the client's client. You need to distinguish between what a client thinks they need and what they actually need.

Why strategy is important

When not built on a strategic foundation, design easily becomes reduced to ornamentation. Although potentially looking appealing, it may actually work

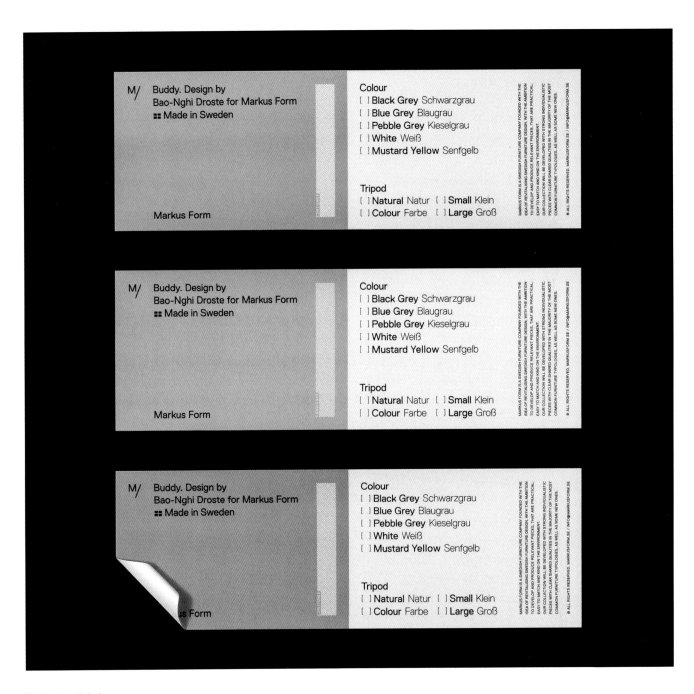

Packaging labels

against the targets the company has set for itself. Only by analyzing the various factors that determine a company's success can we determine the steps that need taken to reach the goal.

The project brief

We provide the client with a set of questions to help them prepare the project brief. This can be done in writing or as a workshop or meeting. Most of our project phases include client reviews, ensuring we're in sync and enabling us to avoid spending too much time working on something that the client would likely have rejected.

From strategy to design

The design community often frowns on using your intuition during the design process. For us, however, intuition plays an integral part in the process. That said, we're only able to make informed choices when we determine what we want to achieve and how to get there. This requires both experience and project-specific research.

In the case of a start-up, there's often one or two people who embody the company. Thinking about a brand as a character can sometimes help when creating a visual identity that aims to avoid the often dull voice of the corporate world. We want to design visual identities that make it easier for people to understand and relate to the companies they represent.

Generating varied ideas

Whenever we feel that we're moving from exploring a concept to exploring details, we try to take a step back and approach the project from a different angle.

To start fresh can be the best medicine to avoid a stagnating process. After doing this a few times, we're able to compare the different concepts and perhaps create a hybrid by combining the most potent ideas from various sketches.

Only by analyzing the various factors that determine a company's success can we determine which steps need to be taken to reach the goal.

Another method that often leads to breakthroughs when we're stuck is to present the work to another team member who's had little insight in the project until that point. It's not always the feedback that's important in these sessions, but more about getting an opportunity to verbalize the ideas that up until then may have been fairly abstract. It's at these times

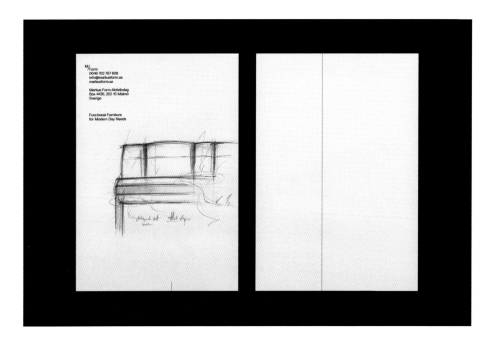

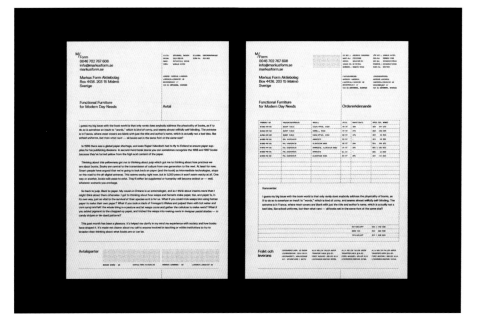

Letterhead with sketch, and with contract order

when it often becomes evident what's worth keeping and what to leave behind.

When to stop experimenting

To determine when a project is finished takes a lot of experience. For many designers, there is always a new opportunity around the corner and learning to identify the right solution comes with years of practice.

In the project's early stages, we define a plan outlining the reasonable time to spend on each of the project's deliverables. However, it's not unusual that time shifts from one deliverable to another during a project, as some tasks will likely be finished in less time than was initially anticipated, while other tasks will need more.

The design rationale

One thing we discussed extensively with Markus Form during the initial phase of the project was that the furniture producer's role in the design process has been downplayed over previous decades. We live in the era of the "starchitect," a time in which the people making the furniture often operate in the shadows of the big name designers. Markus Form wants to restore the balance between the designer and the producer.

We used this idea as a conceptual leitmotif for the visual identity, which is built around a virgule or slash (/), as it is popularly referred to. The left side of the virgule represents the producer (i.e., Markus Form), with the other side being made up of the designers he collaborates with. One side is not complete without the other. This creates a dynamic system that has been used in a playful way

throughout the identity, with the names of designers sometimes being replaced with the furniture typologies that the company works within.

The logotype and typographic system is based around the use of a slightly altered version of the Replica typeface, designed for Lineto by the Swiss design studio Norm. The typeface, with characteristics bearing clear evidence of how it was constructed, aligned well with our idea of a brand that reclaims a lost equality between producer and designer in the world of furniture design.

The identity's color system was based around a restricted palette that Markus Form intended to use for their products.

Avoiding copyright infringement

Looking at the sheer number of businesses setting up each year, it's difficult to determine that a certain solution is unique. Arguably every new visual identity, much like any new chair that's designed, is based, if only loosely, on something that already exists.

We've seen many examples of visual identities, especially isolated logotypes, designed in recent years being compared to similar solutions designed and used in the past. As a designer, or as someone who takes an interest in design, you have to ask yourself whether a good solution should be ruled out just because something similar was used by a long defunct and completely unrelated business some thirty years ago. With the rich resources available on the subject, both in online archives and books, and as a result of the seemingly unquenchable interest in logotype design, almost any shape that's simple enough to work as a brand mark already exists in

M/Form
0046 702 767 608
info@markusform.se
markusform.se

Markus Form Aktiebolag
Box 4436. 203 15 Malmö
Sverige

Functional Furniture
for Modern Day Needs

Markus Form
info@markusform.se
Box 4436. 203 15 Malmö
Sweden
M/

Markus Form
Markus Nydén - Managing Director
Mobile 0046 702 767 608
Email markus@markusform.se
Online markusform.se
M/
info@markusform.se
Box 19 - 360 30 Lammhult
Sweden

[MATERIAL: OLIVE WOOD]

Markus Form
0046 702 767 608
info@markusform.se
markusform.se
M/

Stationery layout

some form. The available resources ensure that these old brand marks stay in the public eye, limiting the possibilities for designers to revisit or use certain solutions. An example of this can be found in volumes one and two of the book *Trade Marks & Symbols* by Yasaburo Kuwayama (Van Nostrand Reinhold, 1973), in which you'll see a few brand marks that are almost identical to celebrated visual identities from recent years.

After all, most visual identities need to be able to function according to a similar set of requirements. As a result, it's usually not so much about the individual asset as it is about the system in which the various assets work together. You may not be able to own a plain circle, but a circle in a specific color may work as a brand mark.

Like most designers, we take pride in knowing our history and in keeping up with recent developments in visual identity design. If we do end up with a solution that's similar to something else, there's usually an intuitive hesitance toward it during the design process, ultimately causing us to question and further examine its originality. This has happened in the past and will surely happen again, generally leading us to choose a different concept or execution of the identity at hand.

The trademarking process is usually handled by our clients' law firms. When we're involved in naming a client's company, we may be more closely connected to this process, but it's generally not our responsibility.

The presentation
We usually present an almost finished solution. This means that we'll develop the concept and execution to a certain degree where, albeit not completely finished, we feel that it represents the look and feel of the final visual identity. This process is informed by previous experiences of having strong solutions rejected by clients because of a lack of understanding of the proposal's full potential. As easy as it is to underestimate a client's imagination and visual literacy, it is also easy to fall into the trap of believing that they will be able to extend complex visual systems based on simple cues. Because the visual identities we design generally place emphasis on the system as opposed to an isolated hero asset, such as the logotype, it's paramount to show the client the full system at play.

The risk of this approach is, of course, spending an extensive amount of time on a proposal that will perhaps not be accepted by the client. This happens from time to time, but we've found that by taking this course of action, based on the feedback from the client, we can quickly pinpoint where we missed the target and prepare a new proposal. Usually this means taking a few steps back to look at the range of concepts we prepared before settling on the one initially presented and basing the new proposal around an altered and further developed version of one of those.

Sometimes if a certain solution requires an expensive licensing fee, or the involvement of a type designer, photographer, or illustrator, we'll take a more agile approach to the project and divide the delivery into several presentations, making sure the client is on board before taking on any further costs.

When creating mock-ups and presentation files, we use Adobe Illustrator, InDesign, and Photoshop. When designing websites, we generally build and present a prototype, as opposed to flat sketches.

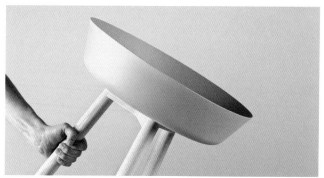

Website and product photography

Number of ideas to present

Normally, we only present one idea to a client. We feel that an important part of designing a visual identity is advising the client on which route to take. Placing this responsibility on the client is an easy way out, and often leads to watered down compromises from which the client wants to cherry-pick and combine various components.

We seem to break the norm in this matter, and we're very clear about our approach from our first meeting with the client. Many clients are initially hesitant, but most of them are quickly won over when we explain the advantages.

Most designers tend to bring their A game when they believe that what they're working on will actually be used, and we're not an exception to that rule. A highly motivated designer will always do a better job than a less motivated one.

Avoiding client micromanagement

When starting a new project, it's paramount that both sides acknowledge that the client is the expert at what they do and we are experts on visual identity design. To be able to work together, both of us need to be respectful and perceptive. Most of our clients are sensitive to this and, though they may suggest changes, these are kept on a more abstract level, allowing us to make the actual design decisions.

When clients don't like the work

When we've presented two separate solutions, with the second one being prepared after an extensive discussion following the initial, rejected proposal, and we still feel that we have a hard time reaching consensus, it may be time to take a step back. This can lead to an internal regrouping on our part, where we replace the lead designer with another member of our team. Sometimes this can be the energy injection a project needs to be able to move forward.

In other cases, we may have to revisit and redefine the original brief before we can return to the design process. In some instances, this requires extending the budget, while in others, it can be kept within the optional correction rounds outlined in the original cost estimate.

Brand guidelines

When we design a visual identity, we usually deliver it with a set of brand guidelines. Traditionally, we deliver it as a PDF document and sometimes a book or booklet. Increasingly we deliver these guidelines in the form of a log-in–based website where all the brand assets are collated and available for download, along with usage guidelines. There are many advantages to this approach, including the employees of the company and potential subcontractors to both test-use the assets and to prepare documents with the right formatting online.

The role the guidelines play varies from client to client, depending on their size and, ultimately, on the qualifications of whoever will be responsible for their communication and marketing. Some of our clients work with advertising agencies or have an in-house department that's capable of not only following the rules, but also of adding value to the visual identity by stretching the limits of the system that we've established. This, of course, allows for a more flexible system.

Art direction for the Buddy table

In other instances, the client's person in charge of the branded communication may be the same person who handles the bookkeeping and prepares coffee for meetings, in which case we will prescribe a stricter system with limited room for errors.

To ensure the work we create is what ends up in use, we like to meet the people who handle the client's communication and marketing. This gives us an opportunity to explain our intentions with the work that we've done and answer any potential questions to avoid misunderstandings. This meeting also allows us to voice any potential concerns we may have with the way the agency or in-house department interprets the visual identity and its guidelines. Sometimes we are also involved in reviewing proposals for campaigns and similar brand exercises, in the capacity of brand guardians.

Measuring success

We hold regular client meetings with ongoing projects to discuss additions to the scope and measure the impact of our work. Some clients have tangible targets that are easily measured and, although there are usually multiple factors contributing to their success, we can often quickly determine whether our work contributed in the way we and our client anticipated it would. This can be measured by an increase in sales or in the number of visitors to a client's website, for instance.

Finding your first clients

Think about your extended network of family and friends as potential clients. Some of our first projects were for friends and for friends of friends. Although they sometimes lack in the ability to pay reasonably for your work, they will likely make up for it in bestowing great trust in you. This will allow you to do projects that truly represent you and how you want to work, hopefully leading to new, better paid commissions that help you to establish a sustainable business model for your studio.

We have always spent a lot of time and energy, and ultimately money, on properly documenting our projects. We can safely say that this has been an important factor contributing to the success and reputation of our studio.

Key points

Remember that as designers, it's not just the client choosing to work with us, it's also us choosing to work with the client.

Know the value you can bring to a project, but also be aware of how valuable the right project can be for your portfolio in helping to attract other, more lucrative projects.

When design isn't built on a strategic foundation, it can easily be reduced to simple ornamentation. While it may look appealing, the result might actually work against the targets the client has set for the brand.

Every new visual identity is arguably based upon something that already exists, much like any new chair that's designed.

Thank you

Northern Ireland
www.davidairey.com

With much respect and appreciation, thank you to the talented designers who very kindly agreed to be interviewed. This book also wouldn't have happened without the trust and support of the fantastic team at Rockport. Thank you, too, for giving me a slice of your valuable time. I hope you've enjoyed reading as much as I enjoyed piecing everything together.

— David Airey

Index